A must read for understanding that when you have an entire organization rallying around and lifting up your organization's higher purpose, that's when the magic happens—that's when everyone associated with your company can THRIVE.

—**Kip Tindell**
Chairman and CEO, The Container Store

We live in an age of paradox. Viktor Frankl taught us that happiness cannot be pursued; it ensues. It is the outcome of living a life of meaning and purpose. Likewise, profits should not be pursued; they result when a company has a noble purpose and pursues it with diligence and caring for human lives. Jackie and Bethany describe their approach as "Savage Thinking." It is in fact deeply human, inspiring, and practical. Read this book to understand how to reinvent your business and align your Purpose with the deepest imperatives of our times.

—**Raj Sisodia**
Author, *Conscious Capitalism & Firms of Endearment*

I love your book title; your message; and your description of how to achieve a purpose-driven organization. Everything that you espouse, Southwest Airlines has tried to embody.

—**Herb Kelleher**
Founder and Chairman Emeritus, Southwest Airlines

This is unifying our leadership around something we can all believe in and bring to life within our organisation. Being able to communicate what we stand for in just one page is something we could not have done without expert guidance from Savage.

—Marc Edwards
President and CEO, Diamond Offshore

Normally viewed merely as fluff or an afterthought delegated to HR, this book moves Purpose front and center as the essential foundation of business success. Jackie and Bethany transform this otherwise intangible topic into a tactical and easily digestible playbook to help any business thrive.

—Jay Steinfeld
CEO/Founder, Blinds.com

Savage took us on a journey to discover our true Purpose and we found it! With our Purpose as our cornerstone, we are now developing and enhancing our culture and brand both inside and outside of our firm. Savage has been a knowledgeable and valuable guide in this exciting and critical adventure.

—Michael J. Hotchkiss
Chief Executive Officer,
Hotchkiss Insurance Agency, LLC

A wake-up call for companies that may already have a great, defined Purpose, but have not communicated it clearly and often to all stakeholders. If you don't define your Purpose, others will *for* you.

—Dawn H. Kelley
President and CEO, Barney Butter,
Barney & Co.

A worthy read. It is so important to discuss the transition to becoming a purpose-driven company and reshape the role of capitalism in America.

—Jack Lowe
Board Chair, TDI Industries

GET YOUR HEAD OUT OF YOUR BOTTOM LINE

AND BUILD YOUR BRAND ON PURPOSE

JACKIE DRYDEN and
BETHANY ANDELL

Oh Deer
PUBLISHING

Get Your Head Out of Your Bottom Line
And Build Your Brand on Purpose

By Jackie Dryden & Bethany Andell

Published by:
Oh Deer Publishing
4203 Yoakum Boulevard, Floor 4
Houston, Texas 77006
713-522-1555
info@ohdeerpublishing.com

This book is available for special bulk purchase discounts. For more information, contact Oh Deer Publishing.

THE LIBRARY OF CONGRESS HAS CATALOGED THIS EDITION AS FOLLOWS:
Dryden, Jackie & Andell, Bethany
Get Your Head Out of Your Bottom Line
And Build Your Brand on Purpose
2016900311

ISBN 978-0-9860811-1-8

Printed in the United States of America
First Printing 2016
Designed by Dahlia Salazar

TO THE INHERENT GOOD IN ALL COMPANIES

Table of Contents

Part Five—FUSE

Part Six—FUTURE

APPENDIX

A: Exercises

GET YOUR HEAD
OUT OF YOUR BOTTOM LINE
AND BUILD YOUR BRAND
ON PURPOSE

Why We Wrote This Book

GREAT BRANDS ARE BUILT ON SOMETHING
MORE POWERFUL THAN THE BOTTOM LINE

After four decades of working with executives, we began to see a shift in the focus of corporate America—a shift away from long-term strategies to a preoccupation with short-term results.

We weren't the only ones to notice. Across the country, people were beginning to talk about Purpose in business—the non-monetary value a company creates in the world. The premise of leading with Purpose (or your *why*) was inspired by the likes of Simon Sinek, Raj Sisodia, and John Mackey—all innovators and authorities on the subject. They proved that though growth and profits are necessary for any business, the country's most envied and influential brands don't lead with profit first. They recognize that profit is an outcome and that true Purpose provides a reason for people to *want* a company to succeed.

But it's one thing to believe what they say, and another thing to put these ideas into practice.

GREAT BRANDS ARE BUILT ON PURPOSE

As branding experts, we know from experience that great brands are built from the inside out. They are much bigger than logos and slogans. *Everything* a company says and does contributes to the building of its brand. Because of this, the actions and attitudes of employees are central to the brand experience. For many companies, especially service companies, you could argue that your people *are* your brand. When your people come together around one meaningful Purpose, you can't be stopped.

Everyone likes to think they have a great culture and respected "brand." However, when we talk with industry leaders about what keeps them up at night, they continually mention people, recruiting, retention, and reputation. Further, Patrick Lencioni (*The Advantage*) and Dave Logan (*Tribal Leadership*) confirmed what we suspected to be true—that most mission and vision statements find their way into employee handbooks or reside on company websites, but rarely generate cultural alignment or guide an organization's day-to-day behaviors.

We argue that brand, Purpose, and culture are, and should be, interdependent. That they build upon one another to shape the greatest of companies.

WE CALL IT SAVAGE THINKING®

There is a wide gap between knowing something and doing something. So we developed Savage Thinking—an ideology and methodology to help companies shift from their bottom-line focus to a Purpose-led business philosophy.

Savage Thinking is not about defining a new direction for a company, or changing the character of its brand—though guiding with true Purpose can certainly do that. Many great companies have led with Purpose from their inception. They just seem to live and breathe it, to the point where it becomes effortless and informal. But with the majority of companies, Purpose has not been articulated from the beginning, has changed along the way, or has gotten lost when companies are merged, acquired, or have a change in leadership. Whatever the situation, Savage Thinking can help to uncover Purpose and provide a guide for transforming your business into a Purpose-led company. We know this because we first put ourselves to the test, and then began collaborating with other companies to help them discover the numerous benefits of uncovering and aligning with their Purpose.

WE ARE REVOLUTIONIZING
CORPORATE AMERICA

Savage Brands has learned that living and sharing Purpose is a powerful catalyst for impacting the lives of people and improving long-term business success, and we are passionate about helping companies wake up to their true Purpose, realize their vision, and practice the values they may have neglected while being fixated on the bottom line.

In short, we are writing this book because we are focused on unleashing the inherent good in all companies and revolutionizing corporate America—one brand at a time.

—Bethany Andell   —Jackie Dryden

PART ONE

Findings

Chapter 1

How America Got Here

MOST CEOs TODAY ARE GOOD PEOPLE RUNNING GOOD COMPANIES. THEY WORK HARD. THEY RUN THEIR BUSINESSES WITH INTEGRITY, TAKE CARE OF THEIR EMPLOYEES, FOCUS ON THEIR CUSTOMERS, AND GIVE BACK TO THE COMMUNITY. SO WHY IS THERE SO MUCH DISTRUST? WHY DO WE LOVE TO HATE CEOs?

It is obvious that the overall reputation of CEOs today is damaged by the harmful behaviors of a very few but very public group of CEOs. Beyond that, leaders today are also limited and affected by a system that considers profits to be a company's core reason for being. In fact, the pursuit of profit often overshadows all of the good that business brings.

Although growth and profits are absolutely essential to the success of a company, the real game-changer is how these are achieved.

Let's get something straight: employees don't walk into the office on Monday morning and ask, "How do I make money for my company today?"

Unfortunately, because of the current state of corporate America, equating success with shareholder value or steadily increasing profits seems to be the only measure by which company leaders are judged. We're operating within a broken system that demands a focus on short-term gains and the almighty bottom line.

It started with the measurement system created for the Industrial Age. During the Industrial Revolution, a business model that focused on the bottom line made sense for measuring factory output and efficiency. Growth and profits were directly proportional to production volume. Industry finances were run just like the machines used on the factory floors: capital and labor pushed in one end, while growth in profits spat out the other in a calculated, formulaic process.

Today, a focus solely on economic outcomes that ignores human needs and values is outdated—but most companies still operate on this model. Companies continue to run modern-day "factories," feeding in human resources and outputting returns for shareholders. But this model is both archaic and unsustainable. It's causing critical issues for every stakeholder of a company.

EVERY STAKEHOLDER STRUGGLES WITH THIS SYSTEM

Executives

Corporate executives endure a barrage of responsibilities and stress twenty-four hours a day, seven days a week. It has become increasingly difficult to lead from "where the buck stops." Business leaders not only face the specific demand of increasing growth and profits, but also juggle pressing issues such as regulatory change, data management, security, technology, performance, expansion, customer loyalty, and the day-to-day struggle of finding and keeping talent.

Business leaders are most often valued for their ability to drive revenues up and costs down—instead of for their beliefs, leadership styles, innovation, customer service, and contributions to society. This system, coupled with shareholder pressure, forces them to make decisions that are good for short-term gains, but may be bad for the company, its employees, its community, and the greater good. What about leaders who want their companies to be the very best they can be—delivering on their promises and continuously improving? Shouldn't growth be an outcome of being a really great company instead of the primary strategy?

Trust is eroded when stakeholders believe their leaders are only focused on short-term decision-making. And while research shows that most executives believe that trust is critical to their effectiveness as leaders, only 18 percent of American workers trust their leadership.[1]

According to the analysis of Nana von Bernuth in the *Harvard Business Review*,

It's no accident that chief executives so often focus on short-term financial results at the expense of longer-term performance. They have every incentive to do so. If they don't make their quarterly or annual numbers, their compensation drops and their jobs are in jeopardy. Stock analysts, shareholders, and often their own boards judge them harshly if they miss near-term goals. And without equally strong pressure to manage for a future that stretches beyond 90 or 180 days, CEO behavior is unlikely to change. Developing a simple yet rigorous way to gauge long-term performance is crucial; after all, in business, leaders default to managing what's measured.[2]

Employees

The unhealthy dynamic that forces a focus on shareholder value alone creates a less-than-ideal working environment for employees as well. When short-term numbers are the priority, the all-too-familiar knee-jerk reactions to a dip in those numbers—downsizing, furloughs, restructuring, overhead cutting, and asset selling—threaten employees' sense of security. They live in fear that their livelihoods are in jeopardy if revenues are not met.

This is especially hard on employees, since the financial goals of a company are usually outside their individual control or influence.

As a result, workers are unmotivated and disconnected from their work, performing out of fear rather than loyalty. In fact, only 29 percent of North American workers are engaged in their work.[3] The remaining majority of workers are concerned with getting by doing just enough to keep their jobs, not on contributing to something more powerful than their own success. Ever wonder how employees feel when they hear terms like, "people are our greatest asset"—as if employees are a thing? Or when companies install a "human capital management system"—making people synonymous with money?

It is proven that disengagement also has negative effects on employee health and family relationships. When workers are under constant stress and go home exhausted with a bad attitude, it takes a toll on their mental and physical health, not to mention the ripple effect their unhappiness has on their families.

This environment promotes competition, not innovation or teamwork. It engenders disloyalty, as employees think, "If my company would hurt my interests to meet a numerical goal, why should I be loyal to it?" Often, employees end up auctioning their time to the highest bidder, and frequent turnover leads to a lack of stability and to disengagement.

Employees are the vital front-line connection with customers and suppliers. If they are not properly trained and connected with something larger and more important than making money, then businesses risk losing them and alienating clients.

And if you treat your employees right, guess what? Your customers come back, and that makes your shareholders happy. Start with employees and the rest follows from that.

—**Herb Kelleher**, Southwest Airlines[4]

Customers

Although it begins internally, this lack of loyalty and security can become an external issue as well. Customers get the sense that companies are largely interchangeable when competitors sell very similar products and services. With nothing but price as a differentiator, their choice to purchase a specific company's offering or to work with one company over another is a matter of dollars, not relationships.

Many start to feel as if they are settling when it is time to make a purchase or do business with a company. In a culture of cynicism surrounding businesses, customers face many of the same emotional challenges that employees do.

Shareholders

With no solid sense of loyalty among customers, employees, or leadership, how can investors be sure of their investments? Almost every public company wants to attract long-term investors, but ends up reacting to its short-term holders.

Too often, shareholders establish volatile, short-term relationships with companies they believe will earn them the best returns for now. Think of the rise of hedge funds and high-frequency trading and what that has done to further the short-term pressures. If there is a whisper of a downturn on the horizon, shareholders bail out, none of them eager to be left holding the bag. CEOs that consistently champion long-term strategies become targets of shareholder activism—it's no wonder corporate America is in this reactionary position.

Here's the danger of the way things stand now: instead of thinking of profit and shareholder value as desired byproducts of doing good business, we think of them as the only acceptable outcome. As stated in *Conscious Capitalism*, "Unfortunately, early economists went far beyond merely describing how entrepreneurs always seek profits as an important goal, to concluding that maximizing profits is the only important goal of business."[5]

Clearly this isn't the best system—it's hurting everyone involved, even those who would seem most poised to benefit.

But there *is* a better way to drive performance and ultimately profits. The quest for endlessly rising shareholder value can be replaced by a focus on something more human, more satisfying, and more beneficial: *Purpose.*

> The day before something is a breakthrough, it's a crazy idea.
>
> —**Peter Diamandis**[6]

Purpose
The true reason a company exists. *Why* **anyone would choose to** *associate* **with your brand.**

Purpose is the foundation for everything your company believes and does. It is what your business stands for, and serves as the heart and soul of your brand. Purpose expresses your **why**, explaining the impact you are trying to make in the world. It could be considered the non-monetary value your business provides.

EXAMPLES:

Google	**To organize the world's information and make it universally accessible and useful**[7]
Acumen Fund	**Changing the way the world tackles poverty and building a world based on dignity**[8]
Tesla	**To accelerate the world's transition to sustainable transport**[9]

Chapter 2

———

The
Perfect Storm

YOU'VE HEARD THE PROBLEM, AND YOU'VE MOST LIKELY SEEN THE
EVIDENCE OF IT IN YOUR OWN DAY-TO-DAY WORK. OUR MISGUIDED
SYSTEM MAKES IT MORE CHALLENGING TO LEAD BUSINESSES EFFEC-
TIVELY—BUT THE TIMING FOR THE BIRTH OF A NEW BUSINESS MODEL
HAS NEVER BEEN BETTER.

As the corporate world struggles with instability and fear, there is a profound need for positive transformation. Right now, the perfect storm of purposeful change is brewing.

You see, the perception of what business should be about is evolving. Many who have spent decades working within our current system —even some of those who helped create the system as it stands—are acknowledging its ineffectiveness in creating long-term success.

The glorification of shareholder value, historically bred into business executives, is part of a movement that was popularized by Jack Welch, former General Electric CEO, in a speech he gave in 1981.

Now Welch, the same man who initiated this change, maintains that the business world has swung too far in that direction. Welch says that the heavy emphasis executives have put on quarterly profits and share price gains was misplaced.

"On the face of it, shareholder value is the dumbest idea in the world," Welch said. "Shareholder value is a result, not a strategy... Your main constituencies are your employees, your customers and your products."[1]

Worse than a "dumb idea," as Welch puts it, for many, the focus on shareholder value and its supporting business tactics are perceived as greed. And no business leader wants to be seen as greedy.

> Any company that focuses primarily on short-term shareholder value will eventually destroy itself. When entire industries do so—as we have witnessed with financial service institutions and US automakers—they can drag the entire country into a deep recession.
>
> —**Bill George**, Harvard Business School professor, former Medtronic CEO, and best-selling author[2]

BACKLASH AGAINST PERCEIVED GREED

Here's the challenge: if business leaders' only goal is to keep shareholder value steadily rising, constantly improving their bottom line, the only possible strategy is to take over an entire industry—destroying competitors and consuming 100 percent of market share. That kind of drive, however, is almost universally perceived as greed. And, even if this were achievable, where would one go from there?

In some eras, being seen as a greedy company or leader would not have been so bad. People's attitudes toward greed tend to cycle from fascination to distaste every few decades, often bottoming out at deep revulsion in times of economic difficulty.

For example, in the 1930s, as the country suffered through a depression, there was a public outcry against greed. In President Franklin Roosevelt's second Inaugural Address in 1937, he said, "We have always known that heedless self-interest was bad morals; we know now that it is bad economics."[3]

The same thing happened in the 1980s, when excesses and inflation caused almost epidemic bankruptcies—the American population lashed out against greed.

Today, those seen as greedy are *personae non gratae* again. In the wake of the recession that followed 2008's economic crash, with unemployment still burdening many families and cities struggling to recover and grow, any company categorized as greedy risked becoming the target of public outrage and scrutiny.

But some companies have found the balance between profiting and dominating their industry space. Their success can be an example for other leaders who want to be perceived as economy builders, not moneygrubbers.

> I think there's such a thing in the business world as a fair profit and ... fair competition in which everybody in the business community is profiting, rather than one particular business sort of gobbling up all of the interests of others.
>
> —**W. Michael Hoffman**,
> Center for Business Ethics at Bentley College[4]

Take a look at Patagonia, a California-based, high-end outdoor clothing company. During the 2012 holiday rush and mayhem, when retailers across the country were pushing out advertisements to convince people to buy more, Patagonia took a different approach. They encouraged their customers to buy *less*. Competitors everywhere were asking the same question: Why on earth would they encourage *less* spending?

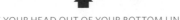

On its company website, Patagonia encouraged sustainability by saying, "We design and sell things made to last and be useful. But we ask our customers not to buy from us what you don't need or can't really use. Everything we make—everything anyone makes—costs the planet more than it gives back."

This sent a clear statement to Patagonia's customer base: We are a company that cares about more than profits. This is not about greed—this is about selling a great product to people who need it and encouraging sustainable behavior. And their customers *love* that about them. Not only does Patagonia's customer base trust the company, but many are also loyal, vocal advocates. People want to invest in brands that have values similar to their own.[5]

Whether you think this action by Patagonia was a stunt or something more, those who thought this would have an adverse financial impact on the company were proven wrong. In the year that Patagonia ran the ad, it doubled revenue and tripled profits over 2008. By proving themselves committed to something bigger than profits, they actually performed better as a company.[6]

In 2015, Jerry Stritzke, President and CEO of specialty outdoor retailer REI, stepped in to disrupt the Black Friday mayhem with a surprising announcement that REI stores would be closed. He stated, "As a member-owned co-op, our definition of success goes beyond money. We believe that a life lived outdoors is a life well lived and we aspire to be stewards of our great outdoors. We think Black Friday has gotten out of hand so we are choosing to invest in helping people get outside with loved ones this holiday. Please join us and inspire us with your experiences. We hope to engage millions of Americans and galvanize the outdoor community to get outside."[7]

The reason that feats like those from Patagonia and REI are gaining notoriety and momentum is because people as a whole are looking for something more powerful, purposeful, and authentic from the companies they work with and buy from. And this shift toward Purpose is being driven by two powerful generations at either end of the age spectrum.

Chapter 3

___

Two Generations

THERE IS AN INTERESTING PHENOMENON HAPPENING RIGHT NOW AS TWO GENERATIONS, AT OPPOSITE ENDS OF THE CAREER SPECTRUM, BRING A SHARED MINDSET TO PROMOTE EXTRAORDINARY CHANGE.

Companies have a front row seat to watch this change in the workforce. While Millennials stream in, looking beyond a paycheck for a workplace that empowers them to make a difference in the world, Baby Boomers are retiring, taking their institutional knowledge with them and becoming more mindful of the wake they're leaving behind.

At the intersection of these two generations there is an incredible opportunity that can only be seized if a company's Purpose and values align and connect with employees on a level beyond the bottom line.

TWO GENERATIONS PUSH FOR PURPOSE

The Millennials: Looking for Meaning

Generation Y, commonly known as the Millennial Generation, encompasses people born roughly from the early 1980s to the early 2000s. The

Millennials have entered the workforce en masse, and are not interested in doing business as usual.

Millennials are not only worried about *how much* money they earn, but also about how they earn it. In fact, they're not satisfied with just a paycheck; they gain satisfaction from their work when they feel they are contributing to something larger and more valuable than the company's earnings. The best and brightest of the new working generation are looking to use their skills to advance companies whose values and vision align with theirs.

This generation's Purpose is not tied to singular, polarizing events like the Vietnam War and civil rights movement of the Baby Boomers' youth. Instead, Millennials' worldview demands more broadly that their lives and efforts mean something. They are constantly looking for a "greater good."

Millennials have high expectations for the companies they contribute to, which means they tend to change jobs frequently when their working environments don't allow them to add value. Many are not finding what they are looking for in any existing corporation, choosing instead to go into business for themselves.

Whether they become entrepreneurs or rise through the ranks of existing companies, these young people are the future business leaders —and they are hungry for a chance to use their influence for good.

The graduating classes from the Harvard Business School sign a voluntary MBA Oath—a student-led pledge—stating, the goal of a business manager is to "serve the greater good." They vow to "act responsibly, ethically and refrain from advancing their 'own narrow ambitions' at the expense of others." They stand for responsible value creation. They aspire to lead the way in setting a higher standard for business leaders.

Similarly, at Columbia Business School, students pledge themselves to an honor code that came from discussions between students and faculty: "As a lifelong member of the Columbia Business School community, I adhere to the principles of truth, integrity, and respect. I will not lie, cheat, steal, or tolerate those who do."[1]

These are examples of attempts by the next generation of business leaders to create a professional code, like the Hippocratic Oath for physicians. Future executives are inspired to use their eventual influence to impact their community, employees, and planet in a positive way.

In the meantime, they're voicing their concerns about how corporations currently impact their employees and their communities.

The Boomers: Leaving a Legacy

At the other end of the spectrum, far removed from their days of graduating from college and entering the workforce, are the Baby Boomers.

This idealistic generation became known for redefining long-held values, and for wanting and expecting the world to improve with time. Driven by a desire to effect change in the '60s and '70s, they set out to revolutionize the world and create a new paradigm of love, tolerance, and acceptance. This group embraced personal freedoms, abhorred big business, and harbored distrust for all things related to the establishment. Their idealism set the stage for future rejections of the status quo.

But somewhere along the way, these aging "rebels" who were going to change the world became part of the system they were fighting to change.

Now, as Boomers face retirement, they are looking back on their long careers and asking challenging questions: What meaningful contributions have I made to the world? What have I worked so long and so hard to accomplish? What kind of legacy will I be leaving? Will the world be a better place because I was here?

They have made vast contributions, but they worry about leaving something behind that has more value than money, and that changes the world for the better. They're reigniting their earlier desire to add meaning to life.

Both the Millennials and the Boomers would surely embrace the words of Owen D. Young, former chairman of General Electric, when he told a 1927 audience at Harvard Business School that "the purpose of a corporation was to provide a good life in both material and cultural terms, not only to its owners, but also to its employees, and thereby to serve the larger goals of the nation."[2]

The combined forces of these groups at either end of the age and work spectrum—as well as the general hunger for companies that are focused on something beyond their bottom line—are opening the door for significant change.

> When the cold front of demographics meets the warm front of unrealized dreams, the result will be a thunderstorm of purpose the likes of which the world has never seen.
>
> —**Daniel Pink**, *Drive*[3]

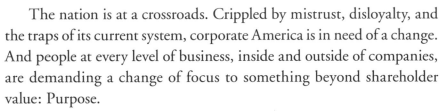

The nation is at a crossroads. Crippled by mistrust, disloyalty, and the traps of its current system, corporate America is in need of a change. And people at every level of business, inside and outside of companies, are demanding a change of focus to something beyond shareholder value: Purpose.

And keep your eyes on the generation that will soon be entering the workforce behind the Millennials, Generation Z. This is how Alexandra Levit described them in a 2015 article in the *New York Times*:

"While a 2015 Census Bureau report found that nearly a third of millennials are still living with their parents, Gen Zers are growing up in a healthier economy and appear eager to be cut loose. They don't wait for their parents to teach them things or tell them how to make decisions." She states that this group is upbeat and full of passion. They are interested in taking an active role in their futures and the communities in which they live, and may be ready to start running things by the time they are 22.[4]

There has never been a better time to think about purposeful business, and replace the traditional desire for *more*—more money, more power, more influence—with a commitment to something more profound.

If you believe that there's a need for a change; if you believe that the Purpose of a company is to provide something of value to the world and make a profit doing it; and if you're interested in knowing more about how purposeful companies attract the best employees, build loyal relationships with their customers, and differentiate themselves from their competition, read on.

PART TWO

Flip

Chapter 4

—

Traditional Thinking

THE TRADITIONAL WAY COMPANIES OPERATE IS IN NEED OF CHANGE. THERE IS A PERVASIVE NOTION THAT PEOPLE MUST WORK HARDER, WORK LONGER, AND DO MORE IN ORDER TO SUCCEED. THE BELIEF IS THAT GROWTH AND PROFITS ARE STRATEGIES, WHEN IN ACTUALITY, THEY ARE RESULTS.

Picture the way most leaders shape their companies, lay out strategic plans, and get work done. They start by thinking about what they do. For most companies, the day-to-day activities of employees are considered the most critical influence on the bottom line and the foundation on which everything else rests. They build strategic plans based on what they do and how to do more. Then, to support these plans, they establish mission, vision, and value statements that tie back, again, to what they do. There are few ways to check for company alignment or measure success against these statements. And all too often, they aren't inspiring or persuasive because they appeal to nothing deeper than being "the number one producer of X" or "the most sought after provider of Y."

Very simply illustrated, traditional business thinking looks something like this:

❶ Write mission, vision, and values that just float in the air— not anchored to anything meaningful

THE BOTTOM LINE

❷ Create a business or strategic plan for growing the company and getting things done

THE BOTTOM LINE

❸ Spend the majority of time and energy in tactical execution—
hoping that the more that gets done, the better the bottom
line. Execution is the only thing touching the line

THE BOTTOM LINE

One problem with this approach is that it breeds the notion that
more is always better—more sales, more products, more offices, more
employees, more work, are necessary for producing more profit. It supports the illusion that the only path to business success is through
getting more done—that this is the best way to increase a company's
value.

The second issue is the lack of interdependence between the layers
of this diagram. Companies go through the process of writing mission,
vision, and values statements only to end up posting them on their
websites, giving them lip service in a few meetings, and then never
referring to them again. These statements don't necessarily connect
with their strategy or how things get done. And every company has
experienced the strategy or plan that never gets executed. After all the
work that goes into these efforts, people usually end up fighting daily
fires instead of directing their attention to the plan or those things that
can have the greatest impact on the business.

Take a look at the following mission and vision statements we
pulled from company websites.[1] They serve as examples of what is
being said in corporate America today. Ask yourself if you believe these

companies are attached to any strategy other than growth and profit? Do you find any of these statements memorable? Do you think they inspire employees, customers, and communities?

"We are a multinational corporation engaged in socially responsible operations, worldwide. It is dedicated to provide products and services of such quality that our customers will receive superior value while our employees and business partners will share in our success and our stockholders will receive a sustained superior return on their investment."

"Guided by relentless focus on our five imperatives, we will constantly strive to implement the critical initiatives required to achieve our vision. In doing this, we will deliver operational excellence in every corner of the Company and meet or exceed our commitments to the many constituencies we serve. All of our long-term strategies and short-term actions will be molded by a set of core values that are shared by each and every associate."

"Our mission is to create consistent value for our customers and supply chain partners that will maximize shareholder value and long-term earnings growth: we will do this by managing our business with integrity and the highest ethical standards, while acting in a socially responsible manner with particular emphasis on the well-being of our teammates and the communities we serve."

"Our goal is to be the most respected global financial services company. Like any other public company, we're obligated to deliver profits and growth to our shareholders. Of equal importance is to deliver those profits and generate growth responsibly."

"Our mission is to be the leading global innovator, developer and provider of cleaning, sanitation and maintenance products, systems, and services. As a team, we will achieve aggressive growth and fair return for our shareholders. We will accomplish this by exceeding the expectations of our customers while conserving resources and preserving the quality of the environment."

"We are a performance driven culture that uses metrics to ensure continuous improvement. Through our distribution and marketing competencies, we provide creative, customized, solutions for our customers. As a result, we achieve superior profit growth as the grocery distribution company of choice."

Our research shows that too many companies are focusing on the wrong end of the equation. They are stuck chasing success through the narrow portal of profit. They do not see how a deeper underlying Purpose can bring people together and move them toward a better outcome. Many companies are mired in a paradigm of paying homage to empty mission statements.

We believe there is a better way to achieve sustainable success— one that flips traditional business thinking upside down. One that starts with Purpose. Because, at the end of the day, it is Purpose that drives performance and performance that drives profits.

Now we're certainly not the first to talk about the power of Purpose in business. But while several of today's best-selling books and popular seminars are helping companies understand the value Purpose plays in business, they generally stop here. Their messages are strong, their arguments are sound, and they may produce a profound desire to improve, but provide no guidelines for implementation.

Recognizing this void, we developed a program for helping companies both uncover their Purpose and discover how to bring it to life.

Chapter 5

———

Savage Thinking

SAVAGE THINKING IS AN APPROACH TO BUILDING VITAL, ENDURING, AND SUSTAINABLE BRANDS. IT OFFERS RENEWED HOPE TO BUSINESS LEADERS WHO STRUGGLE WITH THE INNUMERABLE PRESSURES OF CORPORATE LIFE AND WHO ARE LOOKING FOR A WAY TO LEAVE A POSITIVE AND LASTING BUSINESS LEGACY. IT PAVES THE WAY FOR EXECUTIVES WHO ARE FRUS-TRATED WITH SHORT-TERM DEMANDS AND WANT TO IMPACT THE LONG-TERM SUCCESS OF THEIR BRAND.

We recognize that great business leaders may be hired or start their own companies because they are visionaries. They have a passion for making a difference in the world. But all too often these leaders fall into the trap of managing crises and stressing over the bottom line.

Savage Thinking is an ideology and methodology that not only shares the advantages of connecting with Purpose, but also lays out steps for effecting positive change that benefits all stakeholders.

There are three key differences between traditional thinking and this new ideology. The first is the inclusion of Purpose and behaviors (the missing bookends). The second is flipping traditional thinking

180.° And the third is the interdependence of all phases of Savage Thinking.

These differences represent a dramatic shift away from the "more is better" mindset. They provide the collective benefits of first connecting with your company's Purpose, then outlining the Roadmap for implementation, and ultimately connecting all your words and actions.

THE MISSING BOOKENDS

While most company leaders are proud of their mission, vision, and values statements, they often wonder why people in their organizations do not know, understand, or care about these phrases. Employees feel no attachment to them and cynics don't believe they provide any value at all. This frustrating situation can often be attributed to two missing elements necessary for making these company statements real—elements critical for building a culture that supports its mission, reaches its vision, and lives its values. We call these the missing bookends—Purpose and behaviors.

On one end is your brand's Purpose—your reason for existence. If you do not anchor your mission, vision, and values to a compelling *why*, these expressions will fall flat or fail to inspire. Starting with Purpose serves as ground zero on your journey to building brand loyalty. It helps you earn trust and create positive relationships with each stakeholder group—employees, customers, partners, shareholders, and communities.

On the opposite end from Purpose are behaviors which describe how your values become actionable and manifest into desired conduct. Well-defined behaviors help people understand how they are expected to work together to collectively bring your brand's Purpose to life—every day.

If you do not attach your mission, vision, and values to your true reason for existence, your Purpose, these expressions will hold little weight and generally fail to motivate others. And if you do not attach your values to actionable behaviors, you will have a difficult time building an enviable culture.

Most traditional companies concentrate first on what they do, then create a plan to support more *doing* and establish their identity as the company that *does* X, Y, or Z. While fixating on tactics, they ignore the need for the deeper underlying tie to Purpose.

In Savage Thinking, we start with the FOCUS—*why* the company exists. After that, we develop a FILTER that supports and protects the FOCUS. Then we FUSE all words and actions to help deliver on the Purpose. It's a 180° flip from the way traditional business operates.

THE 180° FLIP

A key difference between Savage Thinking and more traditional approaches to business involves a dramatic shift in focus. It requires you to flip your thinking 180°. Here, you start with Purpose—the *why* that influences all your decisions. This becomes your focal point and serves as the guide for aligning all your plans and actions.

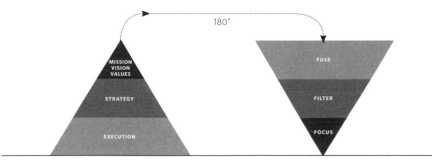

THE BOTTOM LINE

Savage Thinking has three phases. Each phase builds on the others.

① **FOCUS**—*where your truths are uncovered*
A group of truths that express what your company stands for.
Where your energies are focused.

② **FILTER**—*where your truths are examined*
A Roadmap for moving you toward your truths.
Where your decisions are filtered.

③ **FUSE**—*where your truths come to life*
The connector that unifies and makes your truths real.
Where your words and actions fuse together.

The Terms Used in FOCUS
Most of the terms we use in FOCUS are common words. The reason we are sharing our definitions at the beginning of this chapter is because these terms can carry multiple meanings and are being used in various ways in business today.

You may find it helpful to refer back to these as you read through the book. We will explore each term in more detail later.

Purpose
The true reason your company exists.
Why anyone would choose to *associate* with
your brand.

Mission
How you *differentiate* through the way
you deliver on your Purpose every day.

Vision
A vivid picture of where you are headed to
motivate others to take the journey with you.

Values
The unwavering principles necessary
to *infiltrate* your culture with Purpose.

Behaviors
Who you *demonstrate* yourselves
to be through your actions.

After working with more than 200 organizations and spending
more than 10,000 hours in the field assessing top performers,
I know without a doubt that working for a noble purpose engages
top performers in a way that spreadsheets never will.

—**Lisa Earle McLeod**, *Selling with Noble Purpose:
How to Drive Revenue and Do Work that Makes You Proud*[1]

➡ FOCUS

Now, the foundation of the inverted triangle is your FOCUS—the truths that establish *why* your company exists and represents what your brand stands for: your Purpose, mission, vision, values, and behaviors. Throughout the book, we use the terms FOCUS and "truths" when referring to your Purpose and the group of statements that support it.

Understanding and articulating your company's Purpose establishes the point on which everything else balances. This is your true

North, your cause, and your non-monetary reason for being. It describes the value you wish to add to the world and identifies what your brand is committed to making better.

FOCUS provides the foundation for success by directing your attention away from preoccupation with the bottom line to focusing on that which holds the most promise for driving your bottom line up. It is the only part of the inverted triangle that actually touches the bottom line.

> The words "Purpose" and "FOCUS" are frequently used interchangeably throughout this book. Your FOCUS is the set of your Purpose-driven expressions—your truths. Purpose is the foundation for your FOCUS and all of its statements, and the driver of all that follows.

Now, compare the following mission and vision statements with the ones we shared in the previous chapter. Hopefully you will see a dramatic difference. Ask the same questions we posed before. Do you believe these companies are interested in making a meaningful difference in the world or are they more concerned with their bottom lines? Do you find any of these statements memorable or inspiring?

"To bring inspiration and innovation to every athlete in the world."[2]

"To enable people and businesses throughout the world realize their full potential."[3]

"Google's mission is to organize the world's information and make is universally accessible and useful."[4]

"The purpose of Disneyland is to create happiness for others."[5]

"To passionately create innovation for our stakeholders at the intersection of chemistry, biology, and physics."[6]

> I would argue that purpose-driven companies have a huge competitive advantage right now. Employees and customers are hungry for purpose ... We want to feel that our lives have a deeper meaning that goes beyond paychecks and discount shopping.
>
> —**Rich Karlgaard**, *Purpose-Driven Leadership*[7]

➡ FILTER

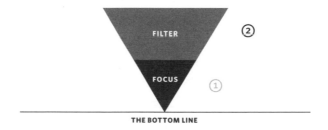

THE BOTTOM LINE

Once your FOCUS has been established, you're ready to create your FILTER. This starts with assessing your relationships and operations to check for alignment, then generating the Roadmap for applying your FOCUS. This phase lays out how your company will function in support of your FOCUS by examining each element of your business.

Strategic plans are nothing new; almost every company writes them on a regular basis. What is different about FILTER is you do an in-depth assessment before doing any planning. Then you can begin creating the FILTER through which all business decisions will be made and define how your company will make its Purpose authentic.

While cultural, operational, and structural changes may be necessary, aligning with your company's Purpose does not necessarily entail turning your entire business upside down—but it will require you to flip your perspective. Be aware that as you go through this process you will find disconnects as well as uncover the ways in which you are already in alignment.

Take a look at the following example of how aligning actions with Purpose worked for Southwest Airlines. Several years ago, as the company was looking for ways to bring in more revenue, a consultant suggested they could make an additional $350 million by simply charging for bags checked by travelers. Now, it doesn't matter what size your company is, $350 million is going to get your attention.

However, Southwest Airlines has a clearly expressed Purpose: to democratize the skies. Their plans and operations support this Purpose, and they train every member of their team to work toward that belief. They align their business decisions with their Purpose, always working to give people the freedom to fly. Adding the burden of bag check fees did not align with that Purpose, so their answer was a clear no.

Instead, they turned to GSD&M, their advertising agency, and asked them to create television spots featuring Southwest's baggage handlers loving their customers' bags. The ads showed big, burly men getting teary-eyed on the tarmac, waving goodbye to the luggage. They expressed the story of their Purpose very clearly.

The response from customers was huge. Over 12 months, the company drove almost a billion dollars in new revenue because they focused on caring for bags instead of charging for them. It was a decision made in alignment with Purpose that paid off in a big way.[8]

Purpose drives performance.
Performance drives profits.

◆ FUSE

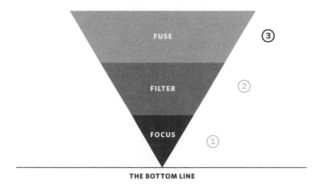

The third phase is FUSE. This is where the rubber meets the road and where you fuse all parts of your company together in support of your Purpose. It is where you demonstrate who you are as a company through your words and actions.

Here the emphasis is on creating, sharing, and living your brand—how you express and demonstrate what you stand for. Because ultimately, it is what your company chooses to say and do, day in and day out, that defines you. A clear Purpose and a brilliant Roadmap won't move your business forward if you can't deliver.

The Savage Thinking illustration is an inverted triangle for a reason. All your words and actions must pass through your FILTER and your FOCUS. Everything must balance on your Purpose.

This helps you prioritize your efforts. It enables you to let go of the notion that you must always do more. It relieves the pressure associated with believing everything is important, and gives you permission to say "no" to doing things that won't further your cause and "yes" to the things that can. It helps you keep your eye on the ball and saves you from getting pulled off course by great-sounding ideas that aren't aligned with your truths. If a proposed action does not pass your FILTER or support your FOCUS, it should be reconsidered.

Roy Spence, one of the founders of GSD&M, an advertising agency in Austin, Texas, talks about a day when he returned home from school with bad marks on his papers in junior high—he was a terrible speller. Rather than scold him, his mother gave him powerful advice: "I don't want you to spend a second of your life trying to become average at what you're bad at. I want you to spend the rest of the life that you've got that God gave you trying to become great at what you're good at."

He asked himself what he was already good at and what he was passionate about. Instead of struggling through the remainder of school trying to become an ace speller, he just did what he loved—writing—and got his ideas down on paper. He jokes that now he has people to do his spelling for him. He gets to focus on what's most important to him, and contribute value to the world in that way.[9]

THE INTERDEPENDENCE

Each layer of the triangle flows down through the next; they are inextricably tied together. Each phase of Savage Thinking touches on an important aspect of your company's brand. In FOCUS, you unearth what your brand stands for. In FILTER, you lay out the Roadmap for demonstrating your commitment. In FUSE, you blend all words and actions to form a culture that both supports and shares your truths.

When everyone in your company understands how their actions reinforce the company's Purpose, you build a cohesive culture where things get done purposefully rather than frenetically. This collective commitment means plans don't end up on a shelf to die. It eliminates the time, energy, and money wasted on initiatives that don't produce sustainable results. It reinforces that the words on your walls actually mean something. And ultimately, everyone at the company works more efficiently toward one common cause positively affecting your relationships with customers, suppliers, partners, communities, and shareholders.

The order is important: first align with your Purpose. This drives employee engagement by connecting them to something of meaning— which, in turn, affects performance and profits. Yes, in spite of this book's title, we are proud capitalists and we love profits. We acknowledge they are necessary for business success and a welcome outcome of building your brand on Purpose.

But beyond profits, this new way of thinking acknowledges the interdependence of all stakeholders and provides value to each group.

> Insanity: doing the same thing over and over again and expecting different results.
>
> —Albert Einstein[10]

Executives

Executives are among the first to benefit from leading with Purpose. The process of uncovering your truths and aligning your business with them is invigorating. We have seen the relief and the reignited passion that executives experience when they reconnect with the *why* behind their company's existence. They are able to see a clear path ahead for the business—a path that lets them move away from stressing over financial minutia and toward big-picture, visionary thinking.

Employees

Employees are a critical stakeholder group. Their attitudes and actions define your brand. Committing to Purpose helps meet the most important needs of employees: personal fulfillment and a sense of belonging. When they fully understand and can share the reasoning behind their work, they feel valued beyond what they are paid. They're more engaged and more highly satisfied, which fosters loyalty. Knowing they have an important role to play in delivering on your company's FOCUS fosters collaboration. When your company acts in accordance

with its Purpose, it generally becomes more transparent and open, which satisfies employees' need for truthful communication and acknowledgment that their efforts are valued.

When a company better meets its employees' needs, those employees are in turn better at meeting customer needs.

Customers

Customers buy from and do business with companies that provide something they need or want. That is the very obvious nature of business. However, when multiple companies offer and deliver similar things, how does the customer make a decision? Sometimes it's perceived value, quality, or an expectation of customer care, all of which are important but most often do not bring sustainable differentiation. Customers feel better about buying from or working with brands they connect with in some way—and it's not just what they know about your product or service—it's also what they feel and believe about your product or service. The delivery, the use, and even how they expect to feel after they use or consume your product or experience your service comes into play. When they connect with *why* your company exists they are elevated out of the typical "features and benefits" orientation and begin to feel as if they are a part of something meaningful. This deeper relationship with your brand adds value to every interaction customers have with your company. It builds love and loyalty for your brand. Think about some of your favorite brands—it really isn't just about the product. This holds true for a company selling to consumers as well as those who sell to other businesses; at the end of the day, it is about engaging people with your brand for a better experience—one that keeps them coming back and sharing their satisfaction with others.

Suppliers

Suppliers and partners are interested in being treated fairly and equitably. In their quest for long-term business relationships, dealing with Purpose-driven companies is ideal. It's much easier for them to build connections with companies whose values are in sync with their own and vice versa. Keep in mind that these relationships can often become an invaluable source for introductions into like-minded businesses and opportunities.

There are many companies who are known for honoring their own Purpose by expecting their suppliers' values and behaviors to align with their own. Starbucks, for example, requires its suppliers to focus on improving conditions for coffee farmers and minimizing negative impact on the environment. They create a mutually beneficial relationship that has helped to propel Starbucks to wild success.

Similarly, Sysco became a world leader in food distribution in part by demanding very high standards from its suppliers, who must meet requirements for environmental, safety, and sustainable practices. Because it values a high level of quality, Sysco educates its suppliers in improving their efforts.

H2H: Human-to-Human

While businesses today are often classified as either B2C (Business-to-Consumer) or B2B (Business-to-Business), we challenge the misconception that these two categories of business are radically different. In both cases, the companies' ultimate goal is to deliver value to people. It's important to note that creating purposeful interactions is not restricted to B2C companies. B2B companies are also trying to reach human decision-makers. We categorize *all* companies as H2H. The realization that all transactions are handled human-to-human prompts companies to consider how their decisions and actions affect people, not just how they might affect finances.

In fact, we argue that Purpose can be even more important in traditional B2B, where relationships and people *are* your brand.

Shareholders

Shareholders can at times be the most difficult stakeholders to satisfy. Most are primarily concerned with profitability, market share, raising

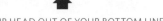

capital, growth, and return on investment. On the surface, Purpose doesn't seem to address those requirements. But when a company has a strong foundation of Purpose, a clear strategic plan, and excellent execution, it becomes more profitable, it increases its market share, and it is poised for growth. And that universally qualifies as satisfaction and shareholder happiness.

With the abundance of hedge funds, high-frequency traders, and dark pools, the financial world is becoming more and more about short-term gains, with very little care about the long-term viability of a company. Most CEOs and Investor Relations professionals we talk to long for the shareholder who's focused on the long term. Declaring and living your Purpose is an opportunity to attract just that kind of investor.

Communities
Societies benefit when a business becomes purposeful. In addition to community outreach, environmental initiatives, and sustainability efforts, a company that is committed to a strong FOCUS provides job opportunities that are more fulfilling and engaging. If employees are engaged, love what they do, and who they do it with, they are happier and healthier. In turn, they take this positivity back to their families and neighborhoods. Purposeful companies are generally considered great places to work. These businesses are sought and welcomed by communities of all sizes.

To see how one successful company honors the value of all stakeholder groups—executives, employees, customers, suppliers, shareholders, and communities—take a look at the Whole Foods website and read their Declaration of Interdependence. Written in 1985 by 60 employees who volunteered to capture the company's beliefs, it has stood the test of time.

Savage Thinking is about committing to and delivering more satisfying interactions with every stakeholder group. These connections promote better performance. And better performance enhances your company's success. It is *not* simple or easy, and completing only part of the process will not produce sustainable results. Remember that the phases are interdependent and each one is necessary for achieving meaningful change.

This new thinking is enabling business leaders to get back to what they do best—envisioning the future with all its possibilities. It is providing an opportunity to inspire others and bring them along on the journey. It's time to get your head out of your bottom line and build your brand on Purpose.

If you're ready to start turning this rhetoric into reality, in the next chapter we'll walk you through the steps.

Savage Thinking in Action

DISCOVERING THE NEED FOR PURPOSE

Executives aren't born with all of the knowledge and skills required to successfully run a company. To be the best leaders possible, they need to be coached, developed, and pointed toward the right leadership opportunities to fit their expertise. That's the job of Moguls, Inc.—a fictitious company headquartered in Denver, Colorado.

More than 20 years ago, John Haley, a whip-smart entrepreneur, saw his peers floundering in new executive roles that overwhelmed them, and he reached out to leading career coaches, HR development experts, and psychologists to assemble a team that could help the executives settle comfortably into their responsibilities.

With charisma and a commanding presence, John was a brilliant entrepreneur who grew the company into a successful firm guiding executive careers: helping companies find the right leaders and helping leaders develop into the executives they wanted to be. While Moguls, Inc. started with just four people in a shared office space in Denver, they had swelled to 400 employees, with satellite offices in Texas, California, and Illinois.

Two decades later, with his hair more gray than brown, John was ready to hand over the reins of the company. He was searching for someone to succeed him, just as he'd helped hundreds of businesses seek out their new leaders. It was a new position for him—and he was confronted with concerns he'd never had to face before.

Nagging at him was the fear that what he brought to the company—what drove him and the business to such heights of success—couldn't be duplicated. Already, with Moguls, Inc. spread over four cities across the country, he found that his influence on the offices had waned, and he could see them start to operate differently than he'd envisioned.

He was absolutely certain that what had made his business work was something that couldn't be found on the company's financial statements. It wasn't something documented in the business processes and service agreements. It was something he couldn't quite put his finger on.

John began to read about leaders he'd admired, people who had built companies that lasted for generations. He talked to friends and colleagues, studied the world's most envied firms, and explored articles on employee engagement and client loyalty.

He was looking for something besides the force of his own personality that could drive the company forward—something that would persist no matter who was at the helm. What he found was Purpose.

Again and again in his investigation, the factor that seemed to tip the scales toward greatness in a company was leading with a strong, well-articulated Purpose that went beyond profits alone. He read that when Purpose was evident in a company's culture every day, not only did a great many "soft metrics" improve—employee engagement and tenure, customer satisfaction, investor loyalty—but that company also delivered stellar financial performance.

He found a company that talked about reshaping businesses in the image of Purpose through a process called Savage Thinking, and he met with their team. He asked dozens of questions, challenged their assertions, and generally kicked the tires on their methodology. Gradually, he became convinced that this was the right path for Moguls, Inc.

John gathered his core team, the three who had been with him since the founding of the company: Campbell, the CFO; Ralph, the EVP of Marketing; and Alex, the EVP of Human Resources. He told them about his concern for the company's sustainability, his succession worries, what he researched, and what he found, explaining why he believed this was a journey they had to take.

"Sounds simple enough," Ralph said. "We've done rebranding before." Ralph was always the first to voice his opinion.

"This doesn't sound like rebranding," Campbell countered. "This sounds like redoing the work we've already done on our mission and vision. What makes you think this is a good investment?"

When John recounted his research and the results he'd seen in other companies, Campbell was mollified, but Alex still seemed unconvinced. "This sounds a lot like what Allison was talking about the other day. And I'll tell you what I told her: I don't think we need this. We already do a lot to engage employees."

John was surprised to hear that Allison, a Senior Consultant who had been with the company for over a decade, had come to the same conclusion he had. She had been on his short list of people inside the company who could replace him as CEO. He asked her to join their discussion, and was pleased with her enthusiasm for the idea of corporate Purpose.

"Businesses *can* have a positive impact on the world," Allison said. "And they should! I think this is absolutely something we should be doing."

There were many more questions from the entire team, but John eventually got buy-in—lukewarm support—from his most trusted executives. They decided to move forward, and John believed that if he and his team fully supported the effort, the entire company could realize the benefits of leading with Purpose.

PART THREE

Focus

Chapter 6

—

Uncovering Your Truths

THERE'S A DISTINCT JOY IN DISCOVERING YOUR PURPOSE. WE'VE SEEN CLIENTS REACH THE MAGICAL MOMENT WHEN THEY RECONNECT WITH THEIR *WHY* AND EVERYONE IN THE ROOM CLEARLY SEES THE TRUE VALUE OF THE WORK THEY DO—EVERY DAY. IT'S EXTREMELY POWERFUL.

That *aha* moment is what you're looking for in FOCUS. This is when you uncover the Purpose, mission, vision, values, and behaviors that will guide every decision going forward.

Now, you might believe that you have already done this important work, that you have a strong mission statement, and you don't see the benefit in going through the process again. That's understandable. But before dismissing the need for additional work, take five minutes to determine whether the leaders of your company are currently aligned with a clear Purpose.

Take a look at the *Five Questions in Five Minutes* exercise. It's a quick, simple, yet enlightening tool that, when answered by your leaders and decision-makers, helps you determine whether there is already

a collective Purpose alive and operating within your company today that is driving all decision making.

All exercises mentioned can be found in the Appendices.

Next, use *The Company Drivers* exercise which has 10 questions that take about 30 minutes to answer. It helps you further examine current behaviors and beliefs at your company, serving as a benchmark as you move forward. Both of these exercises provide good snapshots of your current state and setups for deeper exploration.

Here are two possible findings from these assessment exercises:

❶ On the one hand, you might have had a high level of consensus and uniformity among the responses to the questions posed, *and* every person referenced a higher value to their work than simply increasing profits or shareholder value. This is a great—and rare—place to be. This probably means that you are already living your Purpose! You're the kind of company that the rest of us can learn from.

❷ On the other hand, you might have received a hodgepodge of answers, some of which mentioned purposeful work and some of which referred to money as the main priority. If your answers weren't similar, then you have some important work to do. It's only when all executives and leaders within the company are clear about the *why* of the organization and are able to express it in similar ways that you can begin to align your entire organization around your Purpose—not your bottom line.

If you're in the second camp, with Purpose-finding work to be done, you're in good company—this is where the majority of businesses find themselves. And you're in the right chapter, because accomplishing this is *absolutely critical* for the rest of your efforts to have a lasting impact on your brand.

But before we get into the nitty-gritty of uncovering your Purpose, let's discuss a couple of things that help the process go smoothly.

A FEW HELPFUL NOTES

Be Prepared to be Uncomfortable

This journey is not for the faint of heart. The work you will do in FOCUS is both challenging and stressful, but ultimately exhilarating. Getting your entire executive team on the same page to collectively connect with your true Purpose takes commitment, time, and resources. Be prepared to confront and scrutinize your very reason for existence as a business. And keep in mind, this work cannot be done in a single day because the decisions you make in the discovery sessions will need time and space to breathe in order for you to effectively validate their authenticity. In one experience with a client, when we finally "hit it," he exclaimed that it brought him back to the original reason *why* he went into his field of business in the first place.

Be assured that your Purpose already exists. It may just be dormant—hidden by the constant need to improve, expand, and reach immediate financial goals. Here we are coaxing it out and uncovering how it should lead all your future decisions as a brand—so that your bottom line will flourish as a result.

Keep Your Eyes on Your Own Paper

It's important during this time of reflection that you concentrate on *your* company and *not* the competition. While we know it's tempting to check your answers against your neighbor's paper, so to speak, what works for one company may not work for another. Every business has to connect with its own unique situation. Meaningful success comes from Purpose, not imitation. This process is not about trying to emulate the successes of another organization or position against it; it's about connecting with your company's true North and working to

breathe life into it. It is important to be authentic and not stoop to sameness or comparisons.

Here's the thing about Purpose: by itself, it's not necessarily a differentiator. Many companies may have the same basic Purpose, but differ in how they express and live that Purpose.

For example, take a look at the world renowned MD Anderson Cancer Center. Their Purpose is to eradicate cancer. Obviously, they are not the only hospital striving to cure cancer. But they have made their Purpose so much a part of their culture and their processes, and have embedded it so deeply in their organization's storytelling, it is said that if you ask a gentleman waxing the floors in one of their lobbies what he does for a living, he will tell you he is curing cancer.

Their Purpose—to eradicate cancer—is not a differentiator. But their Purpose in action does set them apart.

That is the real differentiator: the powerful belief shared by all employees at the hospital that what they're doing and the way they are doing it serves the greater good. It changes how their people interact with patients and families; it improves the quality of work done by both medical and non-medical personnel; it even influences the stories that the hospital tells about itself when it recruits and markets—all in service of a higher cause.

So as you're digging deep and revealing the underlying truths for your company, don't ask yourself what your peers are doing. Just make sure what you find is authentic to you and something your people can believe in and act out every day. That's how you set yourself apart in your market.

It Takes Two

We recommend that before you begin this process, find an external consulting partner qualified to help facilitate and analyze your sessions. This process can be challenging and fraught with emotions. People who are passionate about the success of their company may have a hard time coming to consensus about what steps need to be taken to achieve it. Having a facilitator who provides a neutral, outside perspective helps the team through a process that can be very hard to grapple with solely from the inside.

In addition, an "inside" facilitator likely has biased opinions developed through personal experience within the company, or feels the desire to please the executives.

This should be a true collaboration, with both your company and your facilitator aware that neither one can do this alone. It is not about a consultant listening and then going away to bring back answers. An outside firm, facilitator, or consultant cannot ask a few pointed questions and then deliver your Purpose back to you in a fancy folder.

Once you have your partner, you're ready to dive in.

Chapter 7

Discovery Sessions

UNCOVERING YOUR PURPOSE, MISSION, VISION, VALUES, AND BEHAV-
IORS—YOUR FOCUS—CAN BE BOTH INSPIRING AND EXHAUSTING. TO
MAKE THE PROCESS MORE MANAGEABLE AND LESS INTIMIDATING, WE
HAVE BROKEN IT DOWN INTO DIGESTIBLE BITES BY DIVIDING THIS
DISCOVERY INTO SESSIONS. YOU MAY NEED FEWER, BUT HERE WE
WALK YOU THROUGH THIS WORK IN FIVE SESSIONS. THE NUMBER OF
SESSIONS YOU NEED TO ENSURE THE EFFECTIVENESS OF THE PROCESS
MAY BE INFLUENCED BY YOUR BUSINESS COMPLEXITY, DIVERSITY,
GEOGRAPHY, LOGISTICS, TIMING, AND BUDGET.

Regardless of the number of sessions, the work, discussions, brainstorms, exercises, and homework are the same. Obviously, we can't
tell you everything about how to best run these sessions, as they will
change based on your unique needs and circumstances. However, we
offer the following guidance to help you establish a framework for your
important discoveries.

THE GROUND RULES

Use the following ground rules to make these sessions most effective:

- Every session should include key leadership of your company. Once this group is established, everyone needs to be present in every meeting—in person. An ideal size for this group is six to twelve people.

- Meet away from your office and the distractions that come from being easily interrupted. Sessions are most effective when held in a quiet, neutral location.

- Check cell phones and laptops at the door. This time should be spent with total attention to the task at hand. Take enough short breaks during the day to allow participants to check messages and attend to "fires."

- All ideas are equal and have merit, so there is no editing or shooting down the contributions of others.

- No looking to the CEO for answers. The opinions of each person in the room carry equal weight.

- Everyone must come with an open mind and embrace the process. It's important to stay fluid and allow for discoveries and challenges that will happen along the way.

- What happens within the discovery sessions stays within those walls. Maintain confidentiality about individuals' contributions so that everyone feels comfortable speaking his or her mind.

- Leave money at the door. Don't let "money" be an answer or a discussion point in any session. This is about getting to the heart of the value you provide to others.

Between each of the sessions, all participants should be assigned homework to complete before the next meeting. There is a *lot* of material to cover, and big decisions should not be made on the fly. Many of the ideas discussed will need room to grow and time to be digested.

We often recommend several weeks between sessions to allow ample time to reflect, review notes from the meeting, and prepare for the next session. This time between is as important as the meetings themselves. When you're tackling something as large and important as determining your FOCUS, you need time to evaluate each idea's validity and "rightness" for your company. Again, there is no one-size-fits-all solution.

While the final results of these meetings, homework assignments, hours of preparation, and serious reflection will ultimately fit on one page, this could be the most enlightening and impactful assignment your company leadership has ever tackled. When put into action, the words of your FOCUS reach beyond the page and start to shape the language and behaviors of every person in your company.

At the completion of these sessions, your leadership will have a clear idea of your Purpose, mission, vision, values, and behaviors. These form the pivot point on which everything else is balanced and through which all future decisions must funnel.

Here we have broken FOCUS into five sessions.

SESSION ONE—The Set Up

➡ **Prep**

If you are working with a facilitator, you need to gather background materials for that team or individual to review before the first session. At a minimum, this includes an overview of the company's history, research on current industry trends, and all current communications efforts. These materials, along with an analysis of them and an understanding of the company's current landscape serve as background for the questions, exercises, and brainstorming in Session One.

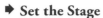
➡ Set the Stage

Begin this meeting by explaining why each person was chosen to participate in this important work. In addition, share the key reasons your company is investing the time, money, and resources on this effort. Discuss your anticipated outcomes and how this discovery is designed to impact every stakeholder, align your culture, and contribute to your future success.

Start with an overview of the Savage Thinking ideology and methodology (pages 25–39) to get everyone on the same page. Then take the group through the agendas for the entire series of sessions so they can understand the full process.

➡ Exercises

If not done before Session One, answer the *Five Questions in Five Minutes* exercise and *The Company Drivers* exercise to establish a snapshot of current expressions and provide a benchmark for future measurement. When these identical exercises are revisited by the same group 12 months after beginning this work, comparing the two sets of answers and tracking changes will show the progression of your company's alignment over time.

Next, use the *High-profile Purpose Matching* exercise to help participants see how well some of the best-known companies in the world are communicating and living their Purpose. Follow this with the *Peer Purpose Matching* exercise, where it often becomes clear that the average company's Purpose is much more difficult to spot. In fact, some companies are challenged even to identify themselves among their peers!

Finally, end this first session with the *Brand Symbol* exercise to help participants visualize and verbalize what the company stands for today and how you see it in a few years.

◆ Discussion

Review each of the exercises used in this session. Pay special attention to areas of agreement as well as disconnects. This should prove to be enlightening. Companies are generally surprised to discover that many of the words and phrases they currently use to describe the business are interchangeable with what other companies claim. Be prepared for a lively exchange as your group discusses where they see your company today and how each envisions an ideal future state. Pay special attention to areas that expose large gaps in points of view and work to bring alignment wherever possible.

◆ Desired Outcome

This is a lot of work to accomplish in a day. Hopefully, the leaders are left with a clear view of both the alignment and the disparity in perceptions existing at your company and in the marketplace at large. This should prompt a sense of resolve to make important changes for better alignment, and a consensus that there is value in doing this work.

◆ Homework

Each participant should consider the drivers, from *The Company Drivers* exercise, that have been discovered and discussed in this session. Which are positive? Which are most important? Why are they and should they be? How can you change those that push the company in negative directions? Be prepared to have a review discussion in Session Two after spending some time reflecting on all that was uncovered in Session One.

All exercises mentioned can be found in the Appendices.

SESSION TWO—Uncover Your Purpose

> **Purpose**
> **The true reason a company exists. *Why* anyone would choose to *associate* with your brand.**
>
> Purpose is the foundation for everything your company believes and does. It is what your business stands for, and serves as the heart and soul of your brand. Purpose expresses your ***why***, explaining the impact you are trying to make in the world. It could be considered the non-monetary value your business provides.

◆ Review

Take a look at the drivers that were discussed in the first session and talk about any new discoveries that participants made on their own after Session One.

◆ Exercises

Use questions such as the following to help the group peel away layers of rhetoric to get to the core of what your company is meant to stand for. The goal is to unlock the foundation that will form your company's Purpose.

- Ⓠ At the end of the day, why do we do what we do and why should anyone care?

- Ⓠ How does what we do impact our customers? Their customers? Their customers' customers?

- Ⓠ What inspires people to come to work here?

- Ⓠ Why should anyone outside our company care about our success?

- Ⓠ What would our raving fans say about us?

- Ⓠ How does/can society benefit from what we provide?

To test your answers and assumptions use *The Five Whys* exercise and continue digging down to the root motivation for your company's existence and its decisions.

An abbreviated example of this type of questioning:

Q **What do we do?**

A We are a law firm.

Q *Why* **do we do what we do?**

A People need attorneys with sharp minds who will treat their legal challenges as if they were our own.

Q **How does this make us different from other law firms?**

A We are more interested in relationship building than billable hours.

Q **How does this benefit our clients and the world?**

A We care about the people who trust in us and we invest in their success. We remove their legal stress. This allows them to stay focused on taking care of their businesses and families.

Purpose (the true reason *why* we exist):

To remove pain and worry from legal challenges.

➡ Discussion

Every person in the room should feel empowered to ask probing questions. When done properly, this session should make some people slightly uncomfortable. But the frustration that arises is the beauty of this discussion. Many times, when you feel the question has been beaten to death, the gem you are looking for is in the next answer. This discussion may take a couple of hours. You will need to keep digging deeper to uncover better and richer answers. Don't stop too early. Continue to push past the obvious to uncover the authentic.

➡ Desired Outcome

While this session is devoted to uncovering your company's Purpose, don't be discouraged if the perfect phrasing for your Purpose statement is not crafted in this meeting. The goal here is not to find the exact, perfect words. If it happens, rejoice! Be aware that most often the actual statement is written in the weeks that follow. Everyone in the room should have a decent idea, though, of what non-monetary reason is at the core of the company. Just remember that this is *not* a tagline. It is an articulation of your belief.

Your outside facilitator can serve as a catalyst for pushing you past the typical, expected answers.

In many instances, companies have Purpose phrases that aren't even related to what they do or sell. For example, Blinds.com's Purpose is about people, not products: *Help people become better than they believe possible.* This describes the company's desire to assist employees, customers, and the world to reach for and achieve more.

➡ Homework

Each participant should use the points brought up in the discussion to draft two to three potential Purpose statements without concern for the exact wording. These will be reviewed in the next session before any final statement is crafted.

We know this is a lot to absorb. But trust us: these sessions should be lively, energetic, and enlightening.

The intense collaboration and resulting lexicon becomes the bedrock for helping your company take charge of your brand and your position in the marketplace.

COMPANY STATEMENTS

We've included some example statements that we love—not for comparison, but for inspiration. They demonstrate how several great companies express what they stand for.

TED
We believe passionately in the power of ideas to
change attitudes, lives and, ultimately, the world[1]

Virgin Unite
We believe business can and must be a force of good
in the world—and that this is also good for business![2]

Bloom Energy
Change the way the world generates and consumes energy[3]

Acumen Fund
Changing the way the world tackles poverty
and building a world based on dignity[4]

Maverick Business
Changing the way business is played[5]

Tesla
To accelerate the world's transition to sustainable transport[6]

Amazon
To be the earth's most customer-centric company where customers
can find and discover anything they might want to buy online[7]

Southwest Airlines
We see a world in which everyone in America has
the chance to go and see and do things they've never dreamed of—
where everyone has the ability to fly.[8]

SESSION THREE—Connect Your Mission and Vision

Mission

How you *differentiate* through the way you deliver on your Purpose every day.

Most mission statements are vague, directionless blurbs of corporate speak that don't inspire purposeful thinking or behaviors. Too much time is spent crafting meaningless jargon, and very little effort is focused on living it.

A true mission statement needs to be an honest account of how well, and in what ways, your business is fulfilling your Purpose. It does not necessarily need to be a single statement. It can actually be a list that describes how you support your Purpose. We sometimes refer to it as Mission support.

➡ Review

Begin with a recap of the previous discussions. Share the draft Purpose statements created by each participant, and then discuss them as a group. Given all the heavy discussions that brought you to this point, you should be able to arrive at a consensus about which statement most closely conveys the heart of your company. Again, don't worry if the wording isn't exactly right—wordsmithing this statement can be done following this session.

➡ Discussion

Next, turn your attention to uncovering your mission and identify the ways in which you differentiate yourself from others. Consider what needs to be done to build your purposeful brand and what truly separates you from your competitors—beyond having great people, innovative ideas, and outstanding customer service. Reach for something more profound, interesting, and unique. Identify any systems, processes, or approaches you have that are not or cannot be easily replicated by someone else. State how you will deliver on your Purpose.

We encourage you to discuss the tangible proof that demonstrates how you are uniquely delivering on the company's Purpose daily. This is a discussion of what is already in place within the organization that supports your Purpose, along with those things that may need to be added, changed, or removed.

➧ **Exercises**

To start defining your mission, ask each member of the group to write four support points for your Purpose. These show how you make your Purpose real. These should not be aspirational, but factual. These are what we like to call "reasons to believe."

❶ Go around the room and ask each person to read his or her list.

❷ Write them on a whiteboard and look for repeats and patterns.

❸ Organize the points into common groups and discuss them.

❹ Combine similar expressions and delete those that are weakest.

❺ Narrow the list down to fewer than five points.

Examine this remaining group of phrases and begin writing a summary phrase or a few bullet-point phrases that encompass the intention of the list. Agree upon the most important one or two that support how you deliver on your Purpose.

Then begin drafting potential mission statements for discussion. Make sure they are credible and differentiating. These options will be refined later and finalized in Session Four.

Vision

A vivid picture of where you are headed to *motivate* others to take the journey with you.

Your vision statement describes where your company will be in the future as a result of delivering on your Purpose. It is an expression of where Purpose is taking the company.

Continued on next page.

> This is a declaration of the best possible outcome for the business, a few years from today. It shares where you envision your company and the world as a result of living your Purpose.
>
> And it is no place to be timid: dream big, be audacious, and gutsy.

Once you have an idea of your Purpose and mission, use the *Sensory Vision Building* exercise to determine what it might look like, feel like, and sound like when your company has perfectly delivered on its Purpose. Vision statements are most powerful when they can be seen, heard, and felt. By evoking these senses, you are able to better help each person connect to how they will experience that moment when the company's vision is reached. This may describe an ideal state that is not fully achievable. But this is fine because vision statements work best when they are aspirational and beneficial to all stakeholders.

➡ Discussion

Ask each participant to share thoughts on the company's vision using questions like these:

- Ⓠ What will the world look like when we deliver on our Purpose?

- Ⓠ Where will our company be in a few years as a result?

- Ⓠ What will others be saying about our organization in several years?

- Ⓠ If someone wrote a feature article about us five years from now, what would the headline be?

These discussions may challenge what has previously been perceived as the vision of the company. As new possibilities are suggested, consider the authenticity and viability of each, and use these discussions to gain clarity on the direction the company should be moving.

◆ Desired Outcome

At the end of this session, the group should have come to an understanding of how the company is supporting its purposeful work and where you would like to be in a few years as a result of delivering on that Purpose. You have established the main support points for your mission, and visualized an ideal future for the company—your vision.

◆ Homework

Participants should review the work done on the company's Purpose, mission, and vision to this point. They should ask, "If this is our Purpose, what does it say about what we value most?" Be prepared to discuss values at the next session.

The facilitator can draft a final version of the mission that shows how the company delivers on its Purpose and craft a vision statement that describes where the business is headed. These will be considered and finalized in Session Four.

Examples of Mission and Vision Statements

TBG Partners (landscape architects)
Purpose: We believe in making the earth a more memorable place

Mission: We create places that encourage the unfolding of life stories

Vision: We partner with other visionaries to help the world appreciate the value of outdoor places and the impact they have on people's lives

Hotchkiss Insurance Agency
Purpose: To provide protection in a world of unknowns

Mission: Our ability to simplify complexity along with our deep desire to serve others allows us to provide customized solutions that help mitigate life's uncertainties

Vision: Because of our drive to protect people, our clients and team members are fiercely loyal to the agency and emboldened to pursue their passions

---

SESSION FOUR—Define Your Values

Values
The unwavering principles necessary to *infiltrate* your culture with Purpose.

Values are at the core of everything your company says and does. They are the set of principles that shape all employee behaviors and serve as the bedrock for the company's culture.

There are several types of values that may exist inside an organization.[9]

Authentic: Real, true and evident inside your culture. These are owned by you and don't sound like anyone else's.

Aspirational: Values you would like to have one day, but are not yet absolute or real.

Pay-to-play: Obvious values that are interchangeable with most other companies.

Accidental: Values a company settles into if it fails to declare true values.

➤ Review

Begin by discussing, revising, and agreeing on a final version of the mission and vision statements. This may take some time, but you can expedite the process by resisting the desire to wordsmith. The final words will eventually come, but trying to create precise statements in a group meeting can be both frustrating and counterproductive. Instead, try to capture the intention of these statements. And remember, these are not taglines.

Once you have come to agreement about how the company supports its Purpose and where the company is headed, you can begin to outline the values that will help your people act in support of your FOCUS.

Values show who you are as a group through what you hold sacred. Expressing your values with verbs instead of nouns is helpful. It is easier for someone to understand how to live a value of "Honor Others" than "Integrity." An actionless noun gives no real indication of how this value is intended to impact behavior.

◆ Exercises

As you start to discuss the values that your company holds near and dear, question what makes them authentic and actionable, and how they align with your Purpose.

Think of your best employees and discuss the traits you admire most in them. If you could clone the ways in which they approach work and enhance your brand, what values would rise to the top?

Use the *Minimal Values Elimination* exercise to get rid of words like "Integrity"—things that are simply standards for doing business and do not elevate or differentiate your business at all.

We've suggested that you keep your company's list of values down to a manageable few, but if your company needs more, don't feel constrained. Many great organizations have quite a few values.

Google, for instance, has ten, listed in their "Ten Things We Know to Be True" document.[10] Another purposeful company, The Container Store, has Seven Foundation Principles.™[11] But what makes them work is that they actually live their values.

As with all of our recommendations in this book, we encourage you to determine the number and type of values that fit your organization and resonate with your people. If they are contributing to a culture that supports your Purpose, they are probably good values.

◆ Discussion

Examine each suggested value, considering which ones define your standard and are authentic to your culture. Choose those that inspire people to contribute and become better. But be careful not to overreach and make these benchmarks unattainable. This will frustrate and confuse both employees and clients.

Discuss whether the values identified are authentic, aspirational, pay-to-play, or accidental. Question whether a value that may be stated as "teamwork" can be expressed in a way that better describes what you mean by this word. Continue working until you have something that feels "ownable" by your organization. For example, "teamwork" may become "honor others," or "be open," or "act as one." Work on each value until it feels authentic and unique to your organization. Southwest Airlines' values are "Warrior's Spirit," "Servant's Heart," "Fun-LUVing Attitude," and "Work the Southwest Way." These embody the airline's personality and define their culture.

➤ Desired Outcome

The participants should have created a list of fewer than a dozen true, compelling, and distinct potential values that clearly express how your culture embodies your Purpose.

➤ Homework

Ask each participant to choose four to six values from the list that they believe are most essential. Write two to three behaviors that support each value chosen. For example, if "Stand Together" is one of your values, a behavior that supports it might be, "Offer assistance to others, even if you are busy."

Examples of Corporate Values

Southwest Airlines (passenger airline carrier)

• Warrior's Spirit	• Servant's Heart	• Fun-LUVing Attitude	• Work the Southwest Way[12]

Disney (entertainment)

• Optimism	• Decency	• Innovation
• Community	• Storytelling	• Quality[13]

Examples of Corporate Values *continued*

Blinds.com (window coverings)

• Experiment Without Fear

• Improve Continuously

• Be Yourself and Speak Up

• Enjoy the Ride[14]

SESSION FIVE—Align Your Behaviors

Behaviors

Who you *demonstrate* yourselves to be through your actions.

How employees bring your company values to life and shape your culture. These should be specific, clarifying, and measurable. They show how employees are expected to conduct themselves to reflect the character of the organization. They describe how employees are expected to act in support of your Purpose, mission, vision, and values. You should be able to reward or fire based on how these are displayed through employee actions and attitudes.

➡ **Review**

Share the homework from each participant, marking those values found to be most important or impactful. Try to narrow the list to three to five core values that truly support your Purpose. Having a short list is helpful as you work to describe the behaviors that support the values. But more than that, a few compelling values are much easier for your people to remember, own, believe, and act on.

Before you begin the exercises on behaviors, write your company's Purpose, mission, vision, and values on a whiteboard for all to see. Everything you ask your employees to do should support these four FOCUS statements.

◆ Exercises

To guide your discussion of what behaviors are needed to support your values, use the *Uncovering Values-based Behaviors* exercise. It will help you identify which are realistic and tangible.

◆ Discussion

For each value you have written on the whiteboard, discuss behaviors to support that value. The goal is to have a few behaviors outlined for each value. Challenge the group to make each behavior you discuss real, actionable, and measurable. You want it to be *very* clear to your employees how they are expected to act. Also keep in mind that any behavior you have outlined for your employees must first be demonstrated by all company leaders.

◆ Desired Outcome

At the end of this session, you should have consensus on behaviors that reinforce each of the values. This is the last component of your FOCUS—and all of your executives must be in agreement and alignment at this point.

Now celebrate! Conclude this final session by honoring the important work accomplished. You have completed a series of challenging and important brainstorms. You are no doubt exhausted, but deserve to feel elated.

Examples of Behaviors

Diamond Offshore (drilling contractor)

Value: Take ownership

Behaviors:
- Run to the challenge
- Deliver on what you promise

Value: Go beyond

Behaviors:
- Solve tomorrow's problems today
- Make it better than you found it

Value: Have courage

Behaviors:
- Challenge conventional thinking
- Speak up, even when it's tough

Value: Exercise care

Behaviors:
- Respect that every action has consequences
- Never cut corners

Value: Win together

Behaviors:
- Learn from each other
- Share success
- Champion a "Culture of We"

YOU ARE HERE

▼ ① **FOCUS:** WHERE PURPOSE IS UNCOVERED

▽ ② **FILTER:** WHERE PURPOSE TAKES SHAPE

▽ ③ **FUSE:** WHERE PURPOSE COMES TO LIFE

Savage Thinking in Action

BUILDING LEADERSHIP'S BELIEF IN PURPOSE

Moguls, Inc.'s full eight-person executive team, now committed to the Savage Thinking process, gathered to begin the journey of uncovering their FOCUS. They filtered into a warmly lit conference room, leaving their laptops and phones at the door with varying degrees of reluctance.

The room was divided. John, Allison, and Wylie, the Managing Partner of Coaching & Training, were excited about the process— John and Allison because they could already envision the positive changes Purpose could make in the company, and Wylie because he loved being on the cutting edge of what's new and next.

At the other end of the spectrum, Paulie, the VP of Career Consulting, believed the team was wasting their time. A full day away from the office for each session? She'd rather be getting something done. Alex, too, still believed that Savage Thinking was something Moguls, Inc. didn't need.

Ralph, Campbell, and David, the VP of Talent Placement, lay somewhere in the middle. Campbell remained skeptical, reserving judgment until the process proved itself. David cared little about the process; he was only interested in the outcome of the sessions and how they would change the numbers he was expected to reach.

Still, the entire group joined in the discussions as the FOCUS work began.

First, the executives looked at their current messages.

- **Their mission:**
  To deliver great value to executives and businesses through superior career advice, training, and placement services

- **Their vision:**

  To be the most highly respected and sought-after firm for grooming and guiding executive careers in America

- **Their values:**

  Integrity, teamwork, trust, and innovation

The facilitator, Anne, noted that they had not established any descriptions of the behaviors required to deliver on any of these statements.

Almost immediately, the scrutiny with which the group was eyeing these statements upset some of the team members, who had been a part of writing them.

"There's nothing wrong with what we have," Paulie insisted. "It tells people exactly what we want them to know about us."

Over the voices of those clamoring to agree, Allison asked, "But are they inspiring? I don't think it's getting to the heart of who we are."

Before the discussion could devolve into argument, Anne began passing out the first of the guided exercises. "Let's do a quick assessment of where you stand now. I'll give you five minutes to answer these five questions. This should give us a starting point for our discussions."

When five minutes passed and the team members shared their answers—with confidence at first, and gradually with more and more surprise at what their peers had to say—the scattered skepticism began to fade away.

It was clear that no two people in the room had the same answers to the questions about what drove their company. One spoke of leveraging expertise, another had written about filling the leadership needs for companies, and a third told of developing their people. Those that were similar were not connected to anything inspiring; they referred to making money and growth rather than any greater Purpose.

A contemplative silence overtook the room. Anne gathered their papers, letting them simmer, before asking them what conclusions they drew from the exercise.

"It's disheartening," John said, looking around the room at his team. "*I* know what I've always seen as the Purpose and the heart of this company. I thought I was building it into the way we worked. But if my own executives don't know…"

"It's why we need to be here!" Allison said. She felt vindicated by the exercise rather than discouraged by it.

Paulie and Alex, who had dragged their feet on the way in the door, expressed their surprise at the disparity between answers, and seemed more ready for a discussion. Still, several around the room held their silence and withheld their judgment, clearly waiting to see what the rest of the session would reveal.

They began to discuss what their true Purpose was as a company, but though they all wished to believe that they were keeping an open mind, many clung hard to the language that populated their existing mission statement.

"This is what we do," David said, somewhat bewildered that the old words were being challenged. "We provide 'superior career advice, training and placement services.' It's… I mean, it's what we do!"

"Yes," said their facilitator. "But *why* do you do it?"

"Because we're the best company at helping executives get where they want to be," David said.

"Yes," Anne repeated. "And *why* be the best at that, and not something else?"

David seemed at a loss, but Ralph jumped in, his voice booming through the room. "Because we have all of the experts in the room who know the factors for what makes a good leader, and how to turn a good leader into a great one."

"*Why*?" Anne asked again.

"We have to, because having a holistic, knowledge-based approach is the only way to put the right people in power in organizations," Allison said, picking up David's train of thought.

"*Why* does that matter?"

That stumped them; it seemed to the team that there were no deeper layers than that. Then Campbell spoke up. "Because we know what a difference it makes when there are really great leaders in the world," she said.

The answer sparked light in the eyes of each of the other executives. As one, they reached the same *aha* moment, and for an instant they experienced the sensation of everyone in the room sharing a collective belief. It was a powerful glimpse into the importance of having a single guiding belief on which they *could* build their entire organization.

Although several of the team members were still not sold on the process, in that moment they began to believe that a collective conviction in something bigger than profits alone could move their company in powerful ways.

That feeling of shared connection and belief persisted through the rest of their discussions that day, and the team left the first session with a renewed energy.

Outside of their cloistered discussions though, away from team members and their facilitator, as the team worked on the post-session FOCUS homework, they began to flounder. Even those who were most excited about the process struggled with finding new words to express the Purpose of Moguls, Inc. They started to revert to comfortable words while still trying to add a new twist to their meaning.

They came to understand how changing beliefs is an ongoing process. It is not like flipping a switch.

CHANGING THE CONVERSATION

As John, Allison, Ralph, Campbell, and the rest of the executive team moved forward with the FOCUS work, several dynamics began to unfold.

Anne pushed them to broaden their idea of Purpose and rework the statements they had drafted as homework—statements to which many of the team members had become very attached.

"I was there when this company was founded," Ralph insisted. "I know what we were trying to achieve. And this is it!" He jabbed his finger at the list of their outlined Purpose statements on the paper before him.

"Maybe that's why *you* came on board," Campbell said, "but it's not why I joined up."

"Keep in mind," Anne coached, "that your Purpose is not only the reason *why* you personally work for Moguls—it's the reason *why* anyone would choose to be associated with your brand."

Allison inserted herself into the conversation. "We all wanted to be associated with this company because of what John built. So *why* did you build it, John?"

All eyes turned to the founder, whose brow furrowed in thought. "I saw people who I knew had brilliant leadership potential struggling to fit into the roles they were handed. I also saw companies pass over people who belonged in a leadership role, and I knew how to make the process better. I was sure that if we brought in experts in HR and psychology and education, we could help companies and leaders find each other. I also knew there was a lot of money to be made for that expertise!"

The team chuckled, and Anne nodded thoughtfully. "You've given a lot of reasons there, John—but I didn't hear an overriding Purpose."

In fact, the more the group talked, the more the session participants realized that, although the Purpose might have been in the background of their founder's motivations two decades earlier, it hadn't been totally clear to him even then, and it certainly hadn't been captured nor communicated throughout the years.

Over time, the company's Purpose had fractured. Anne, hoping for the team to realize the core issue, asked, "We've talked about what you all believe might be the Purpose of your company, but what has been the motivation for your major decisions in the past few years?"

"Profits," Campbell said.

The more the executives talked, the closer they came to the truth that employees had never been clear about their Purpose or how it should impact their daily work. Moguls, Inc. had gotten bogged down in the day-to-day operations, and belief in anything more profound than profits had not been discussed.

Wylie made the problem clear in one simple statement: "Most of our meetings and our communications with the employees are about budgets, sales, growth, and margins. I don't think Purpose really plays a part in our culture at all."

That was the realization the team needed to strip them of the lingering belief that what they had was good enough. Maintaining the status quo—returning to the comfortable language that had described and shaped their company thus far—would not be enough.

Hours into the Savage Thinking process, the team members finally began a more productive discussion about what they wanted their company to be about, and what was realistic.

After much debate and guidance from Anne, they arrived at the Purpose of Moguls, Inc.:

To empower the careers of visionary leaders. This simple phrase captured the overarching benefit the company desired to provide to the world.

Invigorated, they began to tackle their mission—tangible proof of how they were living their Purpose every day at Moguls. Plenty of opinions flew back and forth across the conference table about how the company supported its Purpose. Each executive suggested activities from their own area of expertise as a critical part of their mission.

As they explored, discussed, and rejected dozens of ideas, the team began to wordsmith, attempting to write what were essentially taglines.

"I've got it: 'Delivering top value for top executives,'" Wylie suggested eagerly.

Anne gently reminded them again and again that Purpose and mission were not canned phrases for public consumption—Purpose

expressed what the company stands for and mission supported that Purpose by describing how the company brings its Purpose to life. The exact words weren't important; they only needed to describe how the world would be impacted by what they do.

Allison became the group's "litmus tester," pointing out expressions of the mission that sounded trite or provided no springboard for differentiation. "Does that tell people that we work differently? Or does it sound like everyone else's mission?"

With relief, the team settled at length on their mission:

We are invested in guiding great leaders to acquire the right skills and find the best working environments for achieving their visions. The energy in the room grew as the executives realized they were setting the stage for something powerful.

"I think we're onto something," David said, for the first time shifting out of neutral and expressing real excitement for what they were accomplishing.

Between sessions, Campbell pulled Anne aside. "To be honest," she said, "I thought this whole process was going to be a massive waste of our time. I didn't even think this team would ever agree on one thing—all I could think about that first session was how many hours we were killing sitting in here talking at each other while our phones went off in the other room."

The CFO took a deep breath and smiled. "But we did it. You won me over. This has defied every expectation I had. And I feel like we're moving toward something amazing."

Campbell's attitude shift seemed to mark a tipping point for the group. Eagerly, they moved on to vision, the next milestone.

Anne asked the team to share where they envisioned the company would be a few years down the road. "What would your business look, sound, and feel like as a result of delivering on your Purpose every day? How would you move the needle? What would your employees, clients, suppliers, and community be saying about you? What would it be like to work and do business with Moguls, Inc?"

She continued, "Give as much texture as possible to your vision. Make it bold. Make it specific."

At first, even with the progress they'd made so far, all of their attempts gravitated toward the familiar.

"To be the world's most admired executive training and placement firm," Ralph said. It sounded exactly like the language they'd always used in their marketing materials.

Anne challenged these suggestions. "Ralph, I can feel you settling back into what's comfortable. I need you to think more deeply about the effect you want to have on all of your stakeholders. You want to better the world somehow, not just be admired by it, right?"

After a lively exchange and much massaging of the phrases, the group zeroed in on their vision: *We envision a world where every business leader has a strong backbone, caring heart, and noble purpose.*

ELABORATING ON A COMPELLING PURPOSE

Values came next. Knowing that this session often proved the most challenging, Anne warned the Moguls, Inc. executives, "Don't come into this believing you already have a handle on your values. If you find yourself just defending what already exists, we won't get to where we need to be. We won't discover real, actionable values that resonate in your culture."

To begin, Anne wrote the values suggested by every leader on the whiteboard, and in short order, the entire wall was covered with words. Anne asked if this wall of words described Moguls.

A murmur of hesitant agreement circled the table, with one low answer of, "I guess so," from Ralph.

"All right," Anne said. "Then which of these words differentiates you? Which ones help you achieve your Purpose?"

If they'd been outdoors, the sound of crickets would have been audible in the room. After a moment of silence, Allison said, "Oh wow. This is just the same stuff we have always been saying."

"They just sound like everyone else's," Wylie added.

Discouragement was written on every face at the table. They'd reached a dead end, realizing that the words they had clung to fiercely for two decades were neither sacred nor able to set them apart from their peers. These values didn't form the bedrock on which purposeful behaviors could be built.

"Let's look at what we can eliminate," Anne said.

They began the arduous task of erasing. First, they grouped similar words and removed duplicates. Next, Anne pointed to each remaining word, taking off the board those that were not heatedly defended by one of the participants. Finally—most painfully—they stripped away the words that did not distinguish Moguls, Inc., either erasing them completely or moving them into a list of "parity" values.

The remaining words Anne grouped into "core" and "aspirational" values.

The dialogue was challenging. John, Campbell, Ralph, and Alex, the leaders since the company began, bristled as Moguls' original values—*integrity, teamwork, trust,* and *innovation*—were revealed to be either undesirably vague or common.

Anne counseled the group against including integrity on any list of their values. "Too many companies claim integrity, whether they have it or not. The truth is if you don't have integrity, you shouldn't be in business. Integrity is table stakes."

Reluctantly, the gathered men and women agreed to let go of "integrity." They also observed that "trust" is a byproduct of integrity and blended these together. Integrity morphed into "step up," which encompassed the ideas of empathy, accountability, and the desire to do the right thing.

Similarly, the word "teamwork" became "stand up," which described what they would get from a highly functional team where each member could count on the other to pull his or her weight and have their team members' backs. They believed that "trust" was also covered in this idea.

"Innovation" was the last value to be discussed, and it was the hardest to tackle. David and Ralph argued that this defined their approach to everything they did, and that it was a strong driver of their success. They were reluctant to let this word go and pushed back rather forcefully. It took a while for the two to calm down and even be open to discussing any other option. Anne ultimately convinced them to at least listen to her idea.

Based on their adaptations of the other values, Anne suggested "never let up" as an alternative to the overused word. David agreed that this expressed their intentions: innovation was about endurance in the face of challenges and the understanding that a better answer was always possible.

Ralph, though, pushed back from the table, frowning.

"Everything okay, Ralph?" Anne asked.

"It's just… a lot of change," he said. "I don't know what I expected, but it feels like we're turning everything upside down."

Nods from around the table greeted his statement, although no one seemed quite as overwhelmed as the EVP of Marketing. "What we're doing is hard," Anne acknowledged. "Moguls isn't Southwest Airlines or Google—you have not been focused on the idea of serving a larger Purpose. Any time you have to change something foundational, there's going to be some pain. But what we're doing ultimately is to take what you have—which is good—and we're going to make it unstoppable."

Ralph processed for a few minutes, then rolled back up to the table and folded his hands in front of him. "I'm with you. Let's do it."

The final hurdle for the team to clear was the expressions of how their values would be enacted. Behaviors form the instructions for employees to bring the values to life.

For the Moguls executives, this was less challenging than the previous discussions. It spoke to the practicality in each of them as they answered the question, what does it look like when an employee is acting in accordance with our Purpose?

Ultimately, they defined their behaviors like this:

Step Up
- *Act as if each decision you make affects you personally.*
- *Do the right thing, even when no one is watching.*
- *Follow through on commitments.*

Stand Up
- *Be proud of the value you add and the impact you make.*
- *Pitch in to help others, even when you are busy.*
- *Respond to requests in a timely manner.*

Never Let Up
- *Keep going; use failure as a catalyst.*
- *Take care of yourself and those around you.*
- *Push and grow your abilities every day.*

When the final session ended, the relief was palpable. They had slain the dragon of sameness, stayed true to who they were as a company, and articulated FOCUS statements that would help them make a positive impact on the world.

Celebration and high fives were the order of the day. On every face, both exhaustion and satisfaction were evident.

John was more elated than anyone. Finally, they had something around which they could build the future of the company. They had their Purpose, their mission, their vision, their values, and their behaviors established—they knew what differentiated them, and they had a powerful core that would be a constant at Moguls, Inc., even as leadership changed.

PART FOUR

Filter

Chapter 8

—

Applying Your Lens

ONCE YOU'VE BEEN VICTORIOUS IN UNCOVERING YOUR TRUE NORTH, AND ARTICULATING HOW YOU SUPPORT IT, THE NEXT PHASE IN BUILDING YOUR PURPOSEFUL BRAND IS CREATING A FILTER FOR ALL YOUR RELATIONSHIPS, OPERATIONS, AND ACTIONS. THIS INVOLVES REVIEWING BOTH THE PEOPLE AND FUNCTIONAL SIDES OF YOUR BUSINESS TO CHECK FOR ALIGNMENT WITH YOUR FOCUS—THEN GENERATING THE ROADMAP FOR ACTION.

Although some of the work here may seem familiar, read closely; this is about defining and applying the lens through which you will scrutinize all future efforts. Don't underestimate the power of aligning with your Purpose or the consequences if you don't. The ultimate goal in the FILTER phase is to obtain an accurate snapshot of where you are today and then chart the path forward.

During this phase, you take a close look at the current state of your organization to determine what should be kept, adjusted, added, or removed to build your purposeful brand. Don't get impatient or rush

through this—it may take a few weeks or even a few months. Here are the three key areas that are addressed in this phase:

❶ Relationships: Examine the human side of your business.

❷ Operations: Assess the way you conduct business.

❸ Roadmap: Develop the Purpose Roadmap for moving forward.

In FILTER you ask challenging questions to determine if your existing employees, clients, partners, structure, policies, procedures, products, and services currently support your Purpose. You check for connection points as well as those things that may be barriers or contradictions. Then these findings inform the strategies for building your Roadmap.

If you fail to spend the necessary time and effort here, you will not realize the full impact of the work done up to this point. While it is natural to want to immediately share your Purpose, mission, vision, and values with the world, do not bypass the necessity of creating a strong FILTER.

Without the right relationships and operations to support your Purpose, you risk ending up with words and phrases plastered on breakroom walls that are not a true reflection of what your company believes or how you credibly behave. Your FILTER is the litmus test and guide for all future decisions.

Chapter 9

—

Relationships

TO CONQUER THE DAUNTING TASK OF SCRUTINIZING YOUR COMPA-
NY'S RELATIONSHIPS WITH THE PEOPLE YOU WORK WITH AND FOR, IT
IS BEST TO BREAK THE PROCESS DOWN INTO DIGESTIBLE PIECES.
FIRST, CHECK TO SEE IF YOUR FOCUS STATEMENTS ARE BELIEVABLE
AND CREDIBLE WITH BOTH INTERNAL AND EXTERNAL AUDIENCES.
NEXT, DETERMINE IF YOU HAVE THE RIGHT EMPLOYEES AND THE BEST
MIX OF CLIENTS AND PARTNERS FOR HELPING YOU ACHIEVE YOUR
PURPOSE. FINALLY, TAKE A LOOK AT HOW YOU INTERACT WITH EACH
STAKEHOLDER GROUP.

CHECKING CREDIBILITY

We start here because what people believe can make or break any effort
to effect change. All the hard work you put into finding your FOCUS
will be meaningless if your Purpose isn't believable or credible.
In fact, we can't stress the idea of belief enough: you must connect with
people on an emotional level for them to care about helping achieve

your Purpose. If people don't connect with what you stand for, they won't be interested in advocating for your company's success.

Both internal and external audiences play a critical role in your journey toward Purpose, and they can either support or disrupt your efforts. Without belief in your Purpose, company leaders will neither model the appropriate behaviors nor be committed to spearheading your Purpose initiatives. Employees will not understand why they are expected to behave according to certain values. And clients will quickly discount what you declare you stand for if it does not reflect their actual experiences with your company. Question your stakeholders to confirm whether the decisions your leadership team made during the FOCUS phase resonate with them.

One of the most useful tools for assessing alignment is to conduct short interviews with a few people in each stakeholder group. This research helps determine if others believe you are, or can become, the company described in your FOCUS. Check for support or disconnects by asking smart questions to draw out feelings about your brand.

The questions asked should reflect the ideas brought out during the FOCUS phase, but you're not looking for agreement with the specific wording of your statements since they have not yet been shared outside of your core leadership team. Instead, the questions should capture the intention of your Purpose in multiple ways to gain insights and reactions. You are merely checking for credibility, resonance, and indications of how well your company may already be aligned with your truths.

To get the most trustworthy responses, rely on your third-party facilitator to manage these efforts, and let participants know they will not be identified individually.

Employees
In the internal group you select, include employees of varying tenure, disciplines, and locations. The goal is to get a representative variety of perspectives and check for shared beliefs.

Once the group is selected, prepare a short list of questions. Keep the interviews brief. These conversations can either be conducted in-person, on the phone, or through a survey tool. But whenever possible, personal interaction is preferred because the interviewer will then have the opportunity to reframe questions on the fly or probe more deeply into an answer to gain better understanding.

To help with your question guide, take a look at the kinds of questions TED—a nonprofit that hosts conferences on hundreds of topics in more than 100 languages—might ask of select employees to test the credibility of one portion of their mission statement: *We believe passionately in the power of ideas to change attitudes, lives and, ultimately, the world.*[1]

- **Q** What sets TED apart from other conferences?

- **Q** Do you believe that TED has an impact on the world? If so, how? Why do you believe that?

- **Q** In your job, do you feel you are making a change in the world?

While it may seem repetitive, rephrase your Purpose in several different ways in these questions to get a clear idea of how well people connect with it. Check for affirmation that the Purpose you uncovered is credible and resonates inside your organization.

In this same interview, you may also want to ask questions that specifically target values and behaviors. As an example, the following are questions for measuring alignment with three of Disney's corporate values: community, storytelling, and optimism.[2] These questions are all essentially ways of restating the core question you want answered: Do you believe in what our company stands for?

- **Q** Do you feel supported and encouraged by your peers at work? Can you share an example? (community)

- **Q** Can you recall a time when you or another Disney team member created a great experience for a customer? (storytelling)

Q Do you generally feel positive about your work environment and your future opportunities at Disney? (optimism)

As you can see, each of these questions seeks to reveal whether your core values currently exist in your workplace without directly asking employees whether they believe in "X" value.

In these interviews you can intersperse Purpose and value questions with other, more general questions. This enables you to find patterns that emerge within specific audience groups. For instance, you might want to find out whether employees who have been with the company for many years have a different perception of the brand than new recruits.

Clients

The external group you choose for interviews might consist of current, potential, and former clients. It is good to consider a diverse cross section—long-term relationships, newly acquired business, lost customers, large accounts, small accounts, and a variety of geographic locations. If you have different divisions, locations, or distinct product lines, consider this when deciding which clients to interview.

These questions have less to do with the internal culture of your company and more to do with how those outside your business perceive your culture and value their interactions with your company. You are interested in measuring how well your Purpose resonates with external stakeholders.

We have found it most successful when these interviews are conducted in 15 minutes or less. Don't overwhelm respondents with too many questions. Keep it simple.

For example, based on Moguls' Purpose—To empower the careers of visionary leaders—in conducting these conversations, their facilitator might ask questions such as:

Q How long have you had a relationship with Moguls, Inc.?

Q What is it about this company that made you decide to do business with them?

⊙ Do you believe Moguls "empowers the careers of visionary leaders?" How do they do this?

⊙ If you could clone one aspect of the Moguls culture and share it with the world, what would it be?

⊙ If you could change one thing about Moguls, what would it be?

You are not only checking for credibility of your Purpose, but also learning additional valuable insights for ways to share your FOCUS outside your company walls.

The findings from all of your interviews— internal and external— will help guide the creation of your Purpose Roadmap and inform the development of key messages in the FUSE phase.

THE RIGHT MIX

This section is about discovering whether you currently have relationships with the right people—leaders, managers, employees, customers, prospects, and suppliers. You just completed valuable interviews to determine if people can believe in your Purpose; now investigate further to see if these groups are willing and able to help you achieve your vision.

Without the proper relationships in place, your journey to Purpose will take longer and be a much rockier road. During this phase, you want to gain clarity with regard to the support you have and the challenges you might face. This is necessary for generating an honest snapshot of where you are today so you can plot a realistic path forward.

The sequence is the same for all audiences. First, determine Purpose-based criteria for assessing prospective and current stakeholders. Then, evaluate each group against the criteria to determine how aligned they currently are with your Purpose and how much work you have in front of you.

In practice, the process will differ slightly between employees and clients because each plays a different role. Let's start with one way to assess employee relationships.

Employees

Becoming a purposeful brand is dependent on building a culture with employees who believe in your Purpose and have the values and skills necessary for bringing it to life.

Most likely, your company already has a skills and performance assessment structure in place. We suggest adding a new Purpose and values lens to any existing employee evaluation process.

The following chart offers one way to plot each employee by graphing an assessment of both skills and alignment with the values expressed in FOCUS. (See *Employee Alignment* exercise on page 206.)

Place a dot in the appropriate quadrant for:

 Skills: Does the employee have the necessary abilities and mindset to perform his or her job in a way that will move the company toward achieving our Purpose?

 Values: Does the employee believe in and behave in accordance with our values and behaviors?

EMPLOYEE
ALIGNMENT

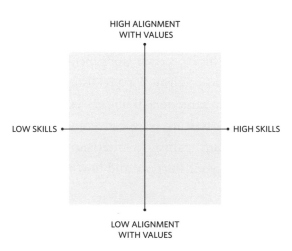

The best employees are those with high values alignment and high skills. It is easier to advance skills from low to high, but more difficult to move people from low values alignment to high values alignment. For that reason, we advise hiring for values and then training for skills.

You can also use a similar chart to evaluate additional attributes such as "clarity" and "desire":

- **Clarity:** Does the employee have a clear understanding of the job and what is expected in this role?

- **Desire:** Does the employee possess enthusiasm and passion for performing the current role?

Assigning a score or measurement for each criteria and determining the minimum acceptable score will help you identify which employees possess the skills and values necessary for moving your business into alignment with your FOCUS.

These exercises are designed to help you examine your workforce's attitudes and abilities, to better understand if you have the right people in the right roles.

At this point we are not saying you have to make any rash staffing decisions, but it is good to know where you might need more work and coaching. This knowledge can also inform any future actions that might need to be taken to address deficiencies.

Clients

Assessing client or customer relationships is as important as evaluating employees when attempting to realize your Purpose. The people you work for and the types of work you do for them directly affect all your experiences, and demonstrate to the outside world what you stand for and believe. Just like the desire to have "right fit" employees, companies should desire to have "right fit" clients. A toxic client can cause major disruption to your culture and stand in the way of servicing your good clients. The best clients are those who align with your values.

In *Nuts!: Southwest Airlines' Crazy Recipe for Business and Personal Success,* there is a story about how Herb Kelleher handled a disgruntled passenger:

One woman who frequently flew on Southwest was constantly disappointed with every aspect of the company's operation. In fact, she became known as the "Pen Pal" because after every flight, she wrote in with a complaint.

She didn't like the fact that the company didn't assign seats; she didn't like the absence of a first-class section; she didn't like not having a meal in flight; she didn't like Southwest's boarding procedure; she didn't like the flight attendants' sporty uniforms and the casual atmosphere.

Her last letter, reciting a litany of complaints, momentarily stumped Southwest's customer relations people. They bumped it up to Herb's [Kelleher, CEO of Southwest] desk, with a note: "This one's yours."

In sixty seconds, Kelleher wrote back and said, "Dear Mrs. Crabapple, We will miss you. Love, Herb."[3]

It takes guts to stand up for what you believe in and turn down those who do not share your values, but it is an important part of achieving your Purpose.

While you most likely already evaluate your clients on a number of financial and performance indicators, it can be beneficial to further scrutinize each customer (or customer group) by using a plus/minus chart to score the relationship. Ask questions such as the following. Then give each company a plus (+), a plus minus (+/-), or a minus (-) to assess their degree of alignment.

- Does the client's culture align with ours?

- Is the client interested in building a valued partnership?

- Does the client trust, support, and believe in the work we do?

- Does the work we do for this company ignite our people?

Q Does this group fit into our market strategy?

Q Does the company respect our values and act with the same behaviors we expect from our employees?

If you are in a service business, another tool for assessing your client relationships is to use a chart similar to the following *Client Alignment* chart. Plot your current customers into the appropriate sections within the arc. Then create an additional chart showing your ideal mix. Moving forward, you can measure your client mix against your initial benchmark.

CLIENT ALIGNMENT

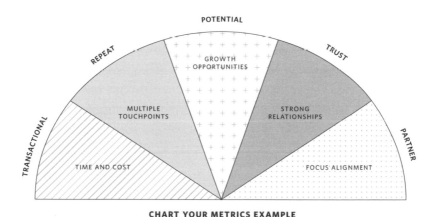

CHART YOUR METRICS EXAMPLE

Partners

Depending on how heavily you rely on your supply chain, consider including your suppliers, partners, distributors, and outside sales groups in these exercises as well. While these groups may on the surface seem less important, they can be instrumental in either helping or hindering your progress. Partnering with like-minded companies can do wonders for propelling you forward on your path.

For instance, think of the reliance Starbucks has on its growers or Ford has on its dealers. The shared values of their suppliers and partners directly impact the brand's reputation.

STRENGTHENING CONNECTIONS

It is good to examine the ways in which you interact with stakeholders across the full lifecycle of your relationships—from how they start to how they end. At each touchpoint, you have the opportunity to reinforce your Purpose through your words and actions. Take stock of how you currently approach all of your interactions, and explore opportunities for more engaging experiences that create value for each of your stakeholders.

Internal

Start with your recruiting activities and think all the way through to when an employee leaves the company. Identify every pivotal moment an employee has with the company. Think through how purposeful each moment is, and if these moments provide a consistent and cohesive experience.

For example, are you doing your best to hire for fit, not just for skills? Are you making promises during recruitment that aren't fulfilled once a person becomes an employee? Does your onboarding process match the employees' day-to-day work experiences? Map this lifecycle to help you see both the hits and the misses your company is making in shaping purposeful experiences.

External

Once you have mapped the employee lifecycle, create a very similar diagram for customers, mapping their entire lifecycle from prospecting to engagement, to delivery, and follow up. As before, you are looking not only for points of alignment, but also for points of disconnect with your Purpose.

Consider how you prospect. Write a clear description of your ideal customer(s). Start with as much detail as possible with regard to the hard facts—size of the business, location(s), industry, products and services, length of time in business, etc. Then take a close look at the human side of your prime prospects and identify the kind of behaviors and attitudes you admire. Also identify how you would like them to treat their employees, clients, and partners. Then describe why these groups would be ideal customers for your company. Reference the *Client Alignment* exercise and check to see if any of your current clients match the descriptions you just completed. Write down which of your current clients are "ideal" and create descriptions based on what they are like. This helps you to create a good target market.

Review how you onboard your clients: is it the same process for every client regardless of size or engagement? Identify the key moments across an engagement. How consistent are these customer experiences? Do the promises you make to a prospective customer reflect the reality of working with your company?

How do you build relationships? What is the experience like of doing business with your company? Does the glow of newness quickly fade or do relationships blossom? Do those groups you actively courted become clients quickly, or become burdens as soon as the contract ink is dry?

Is Purpose evident in all your external interactions? Are there any areas where you might have even greater impact and influence?

Look for potential points of connection and begin courting those companies who fit into your new wheelhouse. Based on these evaluations, continue to identify, seek, and slowly bring new, more aligned relationships into your customer mix.

However, this is not about flipping a switch and instantly changing your entire mix of customers and suppliers. You will likely continue to have business that remains transactional or work with clients who don't fit your ideal profile. We are not suggesting that you drop every customer or supplier whose values do not match yours. We are suggesting that you target your marketing and build relationships with those who do.

In the short-term, financial stability, existing relationships, or important connections may necessitate that you maintain less-than-ideal customers. The difference now is that you start to recognize these companies and begin to move away from doing business with them over time. You want to grow through more aligned relationships and try to limit those which are not.

BUILDING BELIEF

At this point, you might be wondering why we are asking you to create charts and spend time making detailed assessments. First, let us be clear that the previous questions, charts, and graphs are merely examples of the type of work that can be helpful in this phase. They are by no means mandatory nor an exhaustive list of all that you could do. These are here to serve as idea stimulators. The point is to take the time to do this work so that you can be a company that actually "walks your talk."

The ultimate goal of these evaluations is to ensure that every employee, prospect, customer, and supplier who comes into contact with your business comes away feeling as if he or she identifies with your brand and connects with what you stand for as a company.

It is only when you build a workforce that believes in your Purpose, and you align with companies who either have similar ideals or at least understand and respect what you stand for, that you can build a successful brand. When you work with those who are interested in your success as well as their own, it makes these relationships both more enjoyable and productive.

Chapter 10

———

Operations

OPERATIONAL ASSESSMENT IS THE NEXT AREA OF YOUR FILTER TO TACKLE. EVEN THE MOST DEVOUT BELIEVERS IN YOUR PURPOSE WILL BECOME DISCOURAGED IF THEIR INTERACTIONS WITH YOUR COMPANY DO NOT MATCH YOUR PROMISE. ANY LACK OF ALIGNMENT HERE CAN DERAIL YOUR PREVIOUS EFFORTS.

Employees will be more inclined to contribute when they see that your operations and business structure are designed to support what you stand for. The more closely connected your company's operations are with your FOCUS, the more people will trust your leadership and the closer you will be to becoming a purposeful brand.

There are key operational areas to examine as you generate your FILTER:

⭐ Your structure

⭐ Your processes, systems, and tools

⭐ Your product and service offerings

STRUCTURE

First, take a look at whether your current structure reflects your FOCUS. Does it support or hinder your ability to provide purposeful experiences for all stakeholders?

Are there any disconnects? Are the right people in the right positions? Do you have all the right capabilities? What would your ideal structure look like?

To get the ball rolling, consider asking your executive team to independently draw a chart of your current structure. Then gather the input and check to see if you are all starting with the same picture in

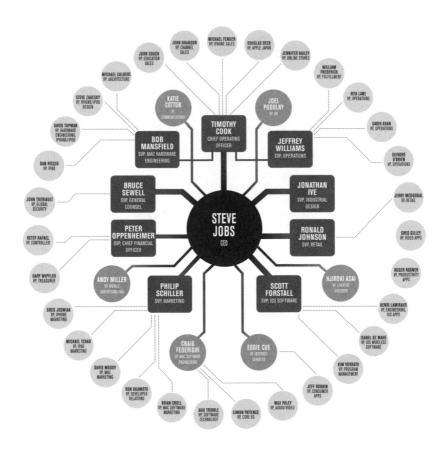

mind. This helps you gain a more accurate representation of your starting place and prompts good debate for moving forward. Next, have them draw the structure they believe will help you achieve your Purpose. These drawings can prompt additional debate and begin to move your thinking forward.

Take time to scrutinize your existing structure closely and challenge traditional thinking as you start to view your organization with new eyes. Look to companies such as Disney[1] and Apple[2] for ideas and inspiration. Their examples are reflections of companies who are better structured for interaction than hierarchy.

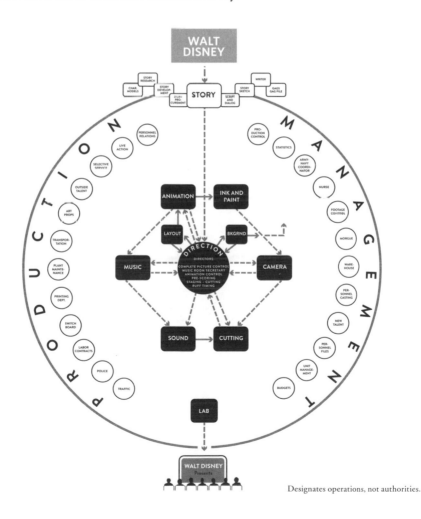

Designates operations, not authorities.

PROCESSES, SYSTEMS, AND TOOLS

Next, take a look at your processes, systems, and tools. This analysis is often overlooked, and many wonder why they stumble when attempting to infuse Purpose into an organization. Just writing or saying the words is not enough. Operationally, make sure there are no legacy systems blocking your efforts.

From business processes to divisions, service lines, or product offerings, examine each major element you have in place. Explore current systems and each business tool you presently use. Do they provide you with the best and most effective path, or is there a better way? Do you have the right management system in place? Do you recruit, train, retain, and reward employees in ways that demonstrate your commitment to your truths? Do your client onboarding, work delivery, customer service, and invoicing processes align? Does everyone in your organization have the tools and resources necessary to support your FOCUS?

For example, we observed the struggle of a company that was working to implement some much-needed behaviors around quality and safety. Unfortunately, their performance reviews promoted time to delivery—rewarding only those projects delivered on time and on budget—which served as a roadblock to the behaviors leadership wanted to promote in the company. The contradiction between what the company said they wanted and what they actually measured performance against caused confusion and strife across the board. No amount of communications could elicit effective change.

Of course, your assessment should go much deeper than just a few questions. The previous are offered to stimulate your thinking and prepare you for the planning process. As you work through the next chapter, Purpose Roadmap, you will lay out the plans for your approach.

A Cautionary Tale

A large organization did everything perfectly for building their purposeful brand—up to the point of evaluating operations. Their executive team spent four full days uncovering their Purpose and all the expressions of their FOCUS. They used a facilitator to conduct internal and external interviews to check the believability of their expressions. And they discovered that their Purpose, mission, vision, and values resonated well with all audiences. They did a preliminary analysis of their culture to check for points of connection and disconnection, and they plotted employee and client groups to establish a benchmark for future evaluations.

But they were unsuccessful at restructuring their organization to align with their Purpose. Operations became their roadblock. The problem was that the business was built through a series of mergers and acquisitions. Each time a new company was acquired, the existing president stayed in charge of that new division and ran it much the same way that he or she had always done. This set up territorial thinking and many conflicting systems and procedures. If one division found a better way of doing something, they refused to tell the others because each division was evaluated by its individual P&L. In many ways, the presidents were in competition with each other. When they refused to change this paradigm or restructure the organization to support a unified company, it became evident that they could not become the company they uncovered in their FOCUS. So they returned to business as usual.

In contrast, when all relationships, offerings, and operations are aligned with *why* a company exists, it builds trust through authenticity. Brands who do this are hard to miss—like Umpqua Bank. This little bank in Oregon decided they wanted to make changes in their communities by becoming more than a place to do financial transactions. Their goal? To become an integral part of the community and provide services that would take them way outside the line of traditional banking. Their strategy led to decisions and actions that look a little out of place for a bank.

Ray Davis, president and chief executive of Umpqua Bank, a sub-sidiary of Umpqua Holdings, said, "Umpqua is always looking for ways to recognize and support the entrepreneurial spirit that drives commu-nity growth. Giving kids lemonade stand supplies and start-up capital is a fun and unexpected way to express our support of small business and community."

Umpqua considers itself more of a retailer than a bank; in fact, it refers to its branches as stores, offering free WiFi access, Umpqua-branded coffee, sewing groups, yoga classes, and movie nights. As a result, they have grown from a small bank with less than $150 million in assets to a strong presence with $22 billion in assets.[3]

PRODUCT AND SERVICE OFFERINGS

Next examine your offerings to determine whether the things you do and sell every day support your Purpose.

Take an objective look at every product and service you currently provide and question whether you have the optimum mix. All too often companies continue to add to their offerings without much fore-thought. It can happen like this: someone comes up with a great new idea for expanding the business, and after a quick analysis, everyone jumps on the bandwagon because it seems like a great way to make more money for the company—at least in the short term. We call this "chasing shiny objects."

As you begin to evaluate whether or not an idea is good for your business, it will no longer be solely a question of how it might impact your bottom line. You will begin to FILTER each decision through your FOCUS.

At TOMS Shoes, their mission is, "With Every Purchase, TOMS® Helps a Person in Need. One for One."[4] Founder and Chief Shoe Giver Blake Mycoskie set out to find a way to put shoes on children who had none. His idea was to let his customers get involved in the process and become benefactors. For each pair of shoes purchased, a pair is given to a needy child. Having a Purpose that is broader than merely selling shoes has allowed them to expand this concept into eyeglasses and so much more. Today, through customer purchases, TOMS helps provide shoes, sight, water, safe birth, and bullying prevention services to people. If their Purpose had been "To be the most admired and respected shoe company in America," they would have limited their ability to expand.

Question how your products and/or services are helping you achieve your vision. Determine which efforts deserve your undivided attention, need to be phased out, or might be missing altogether.

Chapter 11

—

Roadmap

ONCE YOU HAVE CREATED A DETAILED PICTURE OF YOUR CURRENT CULTURE AND OPERATIONS, AND YOU HAVE A CLEAR UNDERSTANDING OF THE IMPLICATIONS OF WHAT YOU'VE FOUND, IT IS TIME TO DO AN ANALYSIS OF WHAT YOU'VE UNCOVERED, FORMULATE YOUR STRATEGY, AND DEVELOP A ROADMAP THAT WILL GUIDE YOUR COMPANY TOWARD ALIGNMENT WITH YOUR FOCUS. YOUR ROADMAP ADDRESSES HOW TO USE THIS INFORMATION TO CHART A PATH FORWARD.

ANALYSIS

After reviewing your culture and operations, you will have a significant amount of data about the current state of your company—so now what?

Summarize your findings to clarify areas of alignment, potential roadblocks, and needs that are currently unmet. Begin to categorize what should be kept, what needs to be refined, and what must be eliminated.

At the end of this assessment, you should have a high-level understanding of your key findings, their potential impact on your company, and how they will influence your planning.

When you uncover any aspect of your company that does not support or is disconnected from your FOCUS, consider removing it or revising it so that it *can* help you make meaningful progress. Don't allow anyone to use the excuse that something has always been done this way to justify a strategy, program, or legacy behavior.

Use findings from the preceding FILTER activities as the benchmarks for reporting on and measuring your success as you move forward.

STRATEGY

A successful strategy reads like a great story, with a clear beginning, middle, and end. Imagine the plot for your company's future and be realistic about what can be achieved now, what might be phased, and what falls into the category of stretch goals—things you want to achieve, but need additional competencies, time, or resources to achieve.

Your company may already have established processes for strategic planning. If you are able to successfully modify them to include Purpose, then by all means, go ahead. This chapter merely offers a few key initiatives to consider and resources that can help you when creating your Purpose Roadmap.

In the relationships and operations assessment you uncovered a snapshot of your company's current state. Now start imagining how to become the purposeful brand you aspire to and outline your plans for living that Purpose.

Take a look at Mayo Clinic, a research hospital that serves more than a million patients each year. Their strategic plan is right in line with their Purpose and sets their operations on the right path.

While most research-focused medical facilities are interested in providing a service and doing good, Mayo Clinic has a larger Purpose

—to transform the experience and delivery of health care. Because their aim is so high, their strategic plan has to reflect their ambitious Purpose while also outlining clear, calculated decisions that support their beliefs. Their winning strategic thinking has helped make them one of the largest integrated nonprofit medical practices groups in the world.

The Mayo Clinic website describes how their unique strategy is directly connected to their beliefs. In June of 2008, the Mayo Clinic Center for Innovation was created to act as a bridge between their medical practice and human-centered design thinking.

The Center for Innovation design research team members come from many different backgrounds, but all share a passion for understanding the needs of people and collaborating with others to design solutions that creatively address those needs.

Designers marry tried-and-true research methods, such as observing patients, interviewing families, and traditional consumer research, with design tools such as visualization, modeling, and prototyping—an approach not common to the healthcare setting.

Mayo Clinic's decision to fuse design principles with a hypothesis-based scientific method is invaluable when uncovering the various human needs involved in the healthcare environment. This unique strategy contributes to Mayo Clinic's ability to create a healthcare experience unlike any other.[1]

Starting with a strong strategy and aligning every aspect of the business with your Purpose is the foundation for a good Roadmap.

Your company probably has an established strategic plan. If not, there are numerous books that tackle how to create these plans in great detail. The difference between traditional strategic plans and a Purpose Roadmap is the Roadmap identifies the highest priorities for getting your company on the path to Purpose. It guides your efforts to gain quick wins and highlights areas of disconnect that pose the most immediate and significant threats to the success of your shift toward Purpose.

It is not meant to be a 50-page document that goes on a shelf, but an overview that can be followed, referred to, and shared in real time.

ROADMAP

Purpose Roadmap
The action plan for making your FOCUS real.

We are not going to take you through the details of creating a Roadmap in this chapter because these plans need to be specific to a company. Each Roadmap is unique and the details should reflect a particular company's path to achieving their Purpose. Instead, we offer a series of questions that your Roadmap should answer in order to guide you toward your vision.

Using the information gathered in your relationships and operations assessments, lay the groundwork for the actions you will take by addressing such questions as:

Relationships

- How will we hire people who believe in our values?
- How do we plan to acknowledge those who exhibit our behaviors and correct those who don't?
- How will we evaluate employees against our values?
- How can we target the right customers?
- What policies and language do we need for attracting the right work and turning down work that does not fit?
- What supplier/partner relationships do we need to be successful?

Operations

- ⓠ What is the ideal structure for supporting our Purpose?
- ⓠ In what areas of our business can we gain the most traction?
- ⓠ How will each area of our company enrich our Purpose?
- ⓠ Where do we need to develop or strengthen competencies?
- ⓠ What additional capabilities are necessary?
- ⓠ What products or services do we need to add, modify, or divest?

Communications

- ⓠ How will we develop core messaging and link all our communication efforts?
- ⓠ How do we plan to roll out our FOCUS internally, then externally?
- ⓠ How are we going to regularly report on new developments and progress?
- ⓠ In what ways will our sales and marketing efforts reflect our Purpose?

This is where you get down to the details necessary for making your truths come to life. It's where you outline what you plan to do, how it will happen, when it will get done, who is responsible, and how much it will cost. It can be helpful to generate a graph, spreadsheet, or chart of your Roadmap so that those responsible for execution can see how their actions fit into the overall picture. Using a graphic Roadmap makes it easier to track your progress and helps to keep people engaged and accountable.

Since this can be an arduous endeavor, we suggest approaching it in stages. Begin by identifying which actions appear to be the most purposeful before discussing how these will each be accomplished.

While it is tempting to quickly dive into tactical execution, make sure you have spent ample time on identifying and evaluating the most effective efforts. Using this phased approach helps to ensure the right things are being done—and done right the first time.

TRUST YOUR ROADMAP

As you move forward in your journey, continually reference your Purpose Roadmap. It is very easy to become caught up in the minutia of day-to-day tasks. Your Roadmap guides your efforts and keeps you on track. This does not mean you shouldn't tweak or revise the plan over time. But it is important to keep it visible and use it to move you through the FUSE phase. By putting your plans into action, and reporting regularly on your progress, you demonstrate commitment to your Purpose and build trust with your stakeholders.

When Savage began the process of transforming into a more purposeful company, we wanted to have a vision toward which we could gear our strategic plan. We knew it wouldn't be enough to write a single sentence that mostly abstracted our Purpose and turned it into this distant, intangible sort of idea.

We wanted something with more meat, more meaning than just words on a wall. After all, values aren't simple, but when you connect values to behaviors, they become clear to people. They can become instilled in a company's culture. But we weren't sure if that could be done with a vision.

Ultimately, we were inspired by Cameron Herold, who has our favorite approach to the idea of a vision. In his book *Double Double: How to Double Your Revenue and Profit in 3 Years or Less*, Herold asks a series of questions designed to help you craft a "Vivid Vision," a vibrantly painted picture of what it will look like when your company achieves its Purpose.[2]

We did something similar for Savage in a grueling, inspiring, intensive process. We generated a four-page document in which we described in emotional but concrete language what it would be like to be an employee, a partner, or a client of Savage. It wasn't just saying "everyone wakes up every day wanting to come to work"—it described *why* they would want to be here and what's happening in our offices every day.

This is a helpful tool for kicking off strategic thinking because it creates a very clear, very vivid goal that every initiative and action plan has to work toward. We highly recommend creating your own Vivid Vision before you start work on your Roadmap or your strategic plan.

YOU ARE HERE

▽ ① FOCUS: WHERE PURPOSE IS UNCOVERED

▼ ② FILTER: WHERE PURPOSE TAKES SHAPE

▽ ③ FUSE: WHERE PURPOSE COMES TO LIFE

Savage Thinking in Action

APPLYING THE FILTER FOR MOVING FORWARD

Once Moguls, Inc. had established their FOCUS, the time was right to develop a strategic plan for enacting Purpose at their company. Here, at least, they felt like they were on solid, familiar ground again. They had years of experience developing strategy and creating plans on their own.

John called Anne, expressing his appreciation for the FOCUS journey. "We're delighted with the results," he said. "And we can see the path clearly to handle it on our own from here. We'll let you know when we start seeing the positive results!"

He held an all-day meeting with his core team of executives, talking through their strategic needs. They already had many of their goals in place for the next one-, three-, and five-year periods, so much of their discussion was simply each executive reporting on his or her status according to existing plans.

Feeling confident, John gave them all the go-ahead to keep chugging along. He expected that with the revised FOCUS statements so fresh in their minds, his executives would make decisions that would push the company toward Purpose. He wasn't sure where he would see evidence of the changes first, but he knew it would probably surface quickly.

But nothing changed.

After three months without even a hint of change in language, operations, or relationships, John reassembled his team.

"What's going on? Where are we on our Purpose?" he asked.

Ralph spoke up first. "Look, John, we've got a business to run. We already know what we're doing—we don't have time to analyze every single thing we're working on like we analyzed those words."

"We agreed on this," John said. "We rewrote everything. Why am I not seeing those changes reflected in the way we're working?"

Alex said, "They're just words on paper. They just don't always connect to what we're doing."

For John it was like a punch in the gut to realize that their entire investment in FOCUS might be in jeopardy, and that the phrases they had so carefully uncovered had become powerless to change his company.

That same afternoon, he called Anne back. "We need a Roadmap," he admitted.

Anne jumped back into the process, helping the leaders through the assessment, analysis, and planning necessary to get the company on track.

At this point, management realized that infusing their FOCUS into the company would be perceived as a change initiative and they should treat it as such.

To begin, Anne worked with Alex to survey their employees and other stakeholders. They determined that while the people who had relationships with Moguls, Inc. were hungry for something meaningful to drive their interactions with the company, they were wary of change. They'd seen several initiatives die on the vine in the past. Many of them would not believe in any change unless they saw it reshaping the structure and policies of the business itself. "Talk is cheap," they said. "We've seen similar efforts launched, and they either failed or just withered away. Before we'll embrace any new change, you need to prove to us that this is different."

So, the executives dove into the operations assessment, turning a critical eye on every piece of their company. They found that much of their structure and systems were already in alignment with their Purpose, but several of their company policies seemed to be working against the kinds of behaviors they espoused in their new FOCUS statements.

Campbell recoiled at the thought of changing the policies. "These are cost-cutting policies that we put in place for a reason," she argued.

"If we change all of these, I won't have any forecasts for what we can expect."

The other executives pointed out that some of the policies encouraged counter-productive behaviors in the quest for lower costs. "We won't allow overtime," Allison said. "But think about the position that puts a consultant in if she's trying to live our behaviors. If she's close to her limit, it means she might not be able to pitch in to help her peer who's struggling with something. Maybe she can't follow through on something she said she'd do because she can't stay late Friday—she has to push it to Monday. Now if she acts according to our policies, she's acting against not one, but two of our values."

They debated finer points of policy, structure, and processes over the course of weeks as they assessed and analyzed different aspects of the company. At times, these conversations veered off track, but always Anne pulled them back with the same question: How is this helping us accomplish our Purpose?

In addition to their operational and structural assessments, they looked critically at their offerings. They found that one of the areas into which they'd been expanding—helping companies fill positions outside of their leadership team—didn't correspond with their Purpose or their vision for Moguls, Inc., and they seriously discussed whether it should be cut.

When it was time to assess their employee and client relationships, Alex and Ralph worked with Anne to develop criteria that would give them a clear indication of which of their current stakeholders could be part of their purposeful brand.

They had their managers perform a new kind of employee review based on these values-based criteria, and overall they were pleasantly surprised by how many of their employees already had high scores for behaving in accordance with their FOCUS.

Alex and Anne profiled the employees that fell below the baseline they had set, and they built a development guide that would help this group better understand, believe, and live the values and behaviors that supported Mogul's Purpose.

The client engagement assessments were eye opening. While Moguls, Inc. did have a few core clients who were beneficial to the company both in their cultural alignment and in their financial commitments, many clients proved to be a hindrance.

Ralph, who had been unpleasantly surprised by this revelation, announced, "I can handle this," and immediately began work on a new marketing strategy that would help them attract the kinds of companies and executives who would be a good fit for Moguls. His intention was to be so clear about their reason for existence that clients would self-select as people and organizations that believed in the same things.

As they moved through FILTER, John made it clear that one of his top priorities for the Purpose Roadmap would be communicating to employees the new criteria they had developed for assessing employee and client relationships. He wanted employees to understand clearly the role they played in moving Moguls toward Purpose. He also wanted everyone within the company to be using the same criteria as they considered how to build and grow relationships with clients.

Based on their assessments, Moguls' leadership developed a strategic plan that addressed the gaps in their business and would build up the areas where they were already making strides.

Some of the items on their list—a shift in their approach to client relationships, changing policies that acted as roadblocks to purposeful behaviors, and implementation of values-based employee assessments—they put into their Purpose Roadmap.

Looking over this final strategy document, John felt the fist of anxiety in his chest loosen. They could make this happen; their FOCUS would be more than just words on paper.

But before they could put their plans into action, they needed to communicate their Purpose so that they could begin to build the belief that would ultimately define and enhance their brand.

PART FIVE

Fuse

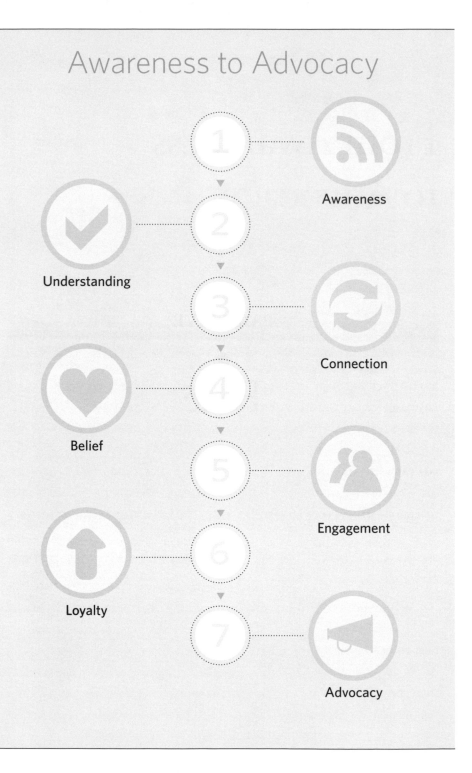

Chapter 12

—

From Awareness to Advocacy

BEFORE WE LAUNCH INTO THE FUSE PHASE, WE WANT TO ADDRESS AN IMPORTANT SEQUENCE THAT EXPLAINS HOW PEOPLE PROCESS INFORMATION AND WHY MANY CORPORATE CHANGE INITIATIVES FAIL TO PRODUCE THEIR DESIRED RESULTS. COMPANIES OFTEN MAKE THE MISTAKE OF MAKING AN ANNOUNCEMENT ONCE AND THEN MOVING ON WITH THE HOPE THAT THE INFORMATION HAS BEEN SHARED AND UNDERSTOOD—THAT SAYING IT ONCE IS ENOUGH. BUT THERE IS A PROCESS THAT ALL OF US GO THROUGH TO ESTABLISH DEEPER, MORE MEANINGFUL CONNECTIONS, WHICH MOVES US ALONG THE PATH FROM AWARENESS TO ADVOCACY.

While most companies profess to want tribal brand loyalty, many are unclear about how to move people along the path from mere awareness to becoming raving fans.

People represent and define your brand, so it is important to bring their heads *and* hearts along with you and ensure they believe and behave in support of your Purpose. To make this happen, you need to demonstrate that what you say you stand for is genuine.

This process applies to all audiences.

❶ Awareness

The sequence begins with telling people what you want them to know. Without awareness, your messages are invisible. This is the most familiar step in the sequence and unfortunately, too many companies stop at this stage. Once they've said aloud or in writing what they want to share, they check communications off their list. Done.

But not so fast! Just because the information has been shared does not mean it reached or connected with your audience, or even reached the intended audience.

❷ Understanding

The second stage in the sequence deals with making sure what you shared is understood. Information can easily get lost in transit between speaker and listener or writer and reader. You want to check that your message was clear and the communications were received. We have all heard a manager say to an employee, "I told you that already." To which the employee responds, "Well, I didn't hear you," or "Well, I must have missed that." Disconnects frequently happen at this stage, and it causes frustration on both sides of the equation. It is only when someone fully understands what you are actually trying to share that people can progress to the next stage.

❸ Connection

Once people understand the message being delivered, they begin to evaluate what they heard or read. They sift through the content to determine what it means for them. Each of us processes information based on our personal experiences and needs. And this processing is critical because the recipients of a message either ignore it, respond out of obligation, or genuinely connect with the information. At this stage, you get people confidently connecting, complying, or merely tuning you out.

④ Belief

Only when you reach the belief stage does your message start to have impact and become trusted. When people are truly accepting of your communication, they think things like, "Yes, I get it. I see the merit in this. I like this idea and believe in what I heard." Then you have an opportunity to build on your message and take it to a deeper level. When people begin to believe in what you share, it starts to become their truth. This is the foundation upon which strong relationships are built. Reaching this milestone propels you into engagement.

⑤ Engagement

Now you have your audience investing time, effort, or resources into your idea. And people are saying, "OK, I'll give this a shot and see how it goes." "I want to try this out." They believe in what you shared and think it might be of benefit to them. In this trial stage, you have made a compelling enough argument to convince people to act on, follow, or support your message.

⑥ Loyalty

At the loyalty stage, alignment begins to take shape. People move from trial engagement to being satisfied with the results of their efforts. They trust both you and your messages. They are willing to pay close attention to future communications. You held up your end of

the bargain and proved that what you have to offer is valuable to them. You earn allegiance because their experience matches the message—and they are willing to stay engaged. They are the employees who can't be poached from your company. These are the customers who keep buying from you. This is where the love begins.

❼ Advocacy

Advocacy is your out-of-the-ballpark home run. Once you have communicated, been understood, passed evaluations, engendered belief, inspired engagement, and built loyalty, people start to become advocates for you, your ideas, and your brand. You forge deep connections that generally defy logic. Emotional commitments are powerful, and this is where people become your raving fans, your brand ambassadors, your tribe, and your champions. They amplify your voice and increase your impact exponentially. This stage of the sequence is the hallmark of the most admired and loved brands—those who continually bring their audiences along in concert with their Purpose, connect with what people believe, and match experiences with what they promise. Advocates start telling your story for you. They are the ones who support and defend your brand at all costs.

This same process applies to all forms of brand communications from business messages to social interactions. You must be heard, understood, and believed before you can breed the deep and enduring connections that result in tribal loyalty.

Chapter 13

Becoming A Purposeful Brand

THE TITLE OF THIS BOOK REFERENCES THE IDEA OF BUILDING A BRAND. THROUGHOUT, WHEN WE TALK ABOUT CHANGE INITIATIVES—STRUCTURAL, CULTURAL, AND BEHAVIORAL—THAT MAY NEED TO TAKE PLACE IN YOUR COMPANY, WE ARE IN ESSENCE TALKING ABOUT "BRANDING," BECAUSE EVERY ASPECT OF YOUR BUSINESS SHAPES YOUR BRAND. BUILDING A "PURPOSEFUL BRAND" IS NOT ABOUT CHANGING YOUR LOGO OR REWRITING YOUR TAGLINE—IT IS ABOUT SHAPING THE EXPERIENCE THAT EVERY STAKEHOLDER HAS WITH YOUR COMPANY.

So if you're wondering where branding comes in, wonder no more—you're in it. Uncovering your Purpose, building a strategy around it, and using it to nurture relationships with employees, customers, suppliers, investors, and every other stakeholder at every level of your company *is* your branding.

Brand
The sum of the perceptions of a product or company.

A brand is how others experience your company emotionally, visually, and through products and interactions. It is the sum total of the personality and perceptions that make up what a company is seen to be. A company's marketing and PR efforts contribute to its brand, as well as its performance, its community involvement, its visual identity, its hiring practices, its employee perks, its investor communications—every decision that the company and its employees make influences public perception of the company.

Up to this point, you have defined your FOCUS and created a FILTER for turning your valuable time, talents, and resources toward purposeful activities. Now you have arrived at the phase where you begin shaping, sharing, and syncing your stories and experiences. The FUSE phase involves making sure that everything your company says and does is in concert with your Purpose. It is only when you FUSE all your messages and actions together that you can build trust.

The success of everything you have done up to this point depends on how well your story is told. You want to substantiate the intrinsic connection between everything you say and all that you do to deliver something of value to the world.

Your company's story communicates your beliefs and your competitive position. It helps employees connect with a compelling reason to come in to work every day. It tells and shows people why they should work for your company, partner with it, buy from it, support it, champion it, and invest in it. When what you do syncs up with what you say, your brand stands for something real in this world.

The founder of Savage Brands, Paula Savage Hansen, defines branding in this way: "Branding is the entire experience you have with a company. While your logo, what you say, and how you present yourself all contribute to your image, branding goes further. The essence of your brand is what you represent—your goals, your vision, and your Purpose. Your brand is not just what's on the outside, but more importantly, what's on the inside."

Chapter 14

———

Shape
Your Story

YOU HAVE PUT VALUABLE TIME AND EFFORT INTO IDENTIFYING YOUR
COMPANY'S FOCUS—YOUR PURPOSE, MISSION, VISION, VALUES, AND
BEHAVIORS. AS THESE MOST LIKELY DIFFER FROM YOUR ORIGINAL
MISSION, VISION, OR VALUE STATEMENTS, YOUR CORE BRAND MES-
SAGES WILL NEED TO ADJUST AS WELL.

While the specifics of how you craft your company story will vary
based on your resources and your Purpose Roadmap, there are several
fundamental elements of purposeful communication that cross all
channels and media. This part of the journey begins with getting your
arms around your authentic story, matching your narrative with your
image, and then following through with flawless execution. These elements collectively impact the quality and effectiveness of all your
communications, moving people along the path from awareness to
advocacy.

Each of your stakeholder audiences (internal and external) has his
or her own needs. Before you begin outlining your story, consider how
your Purpose and mission connect with these needs. Remember, when

defining your mission in FOCUS, you were describing those things that help to differentiate your company. Reference these when developing your story by connecting what you stand for with what the world desires.

Start this process by asking such questions as:

- Given our Purpose, what are the most important things we need to communicate about our company?

- What do our audiences care most about?

- How does our Purpose affect each stakeholder group?

- How do the solutions we offer benefit others?

When developing and sharing your brand story, consider these things: your sequence, concept, message, image, and resources. Each of these plays a part in helping to communicate both cohesively and effectively.

YOUR SEQUENCE

In *Start With Why*, Simon Sinek shares the importance of building your messages by starting with *why*. He says, "A marketing message from Apple, if it were like everyone else's, might sound like this: We make great computers. They're beautifully designed, simple to use and user-friendly. Wanna buy one?" Then he continues to explain that instead, Apple starts their messaging with *why*—that they connect at the belief level by saying something like this: "Everything we do, we believe in challenging the status quo. We believe in thinking differently. The way we challenge the status quo is by making our products beautifully designed, simple to use and user-friendly. And we happen to make great computers. Wanna buy one?"[1] There is a different feel to the second message. It lets the audience know what the company cares about before they are asked to consider buying anything. It allows people to connect with something more powerful than just features, benefits, or price. Messages that start with *why* are more compelling and effective. They connect on an emotional level, attaching to what people believe, before attempting to provide rational support. Remember this as you begin to develop your story.

YOUR CONCEPT

Effective communications start with a powerful idea. Before you begin, stop and think about how to frame what you want to communicate. Consider what you want the audience to understand, feel, and do—and why they should care. This step is often overlooked as people jump right into composing messages.

You need a compelling concept to fuel your brand story. If there is no overarching idea framing your message, it will fail to reach its potential. Too often companies spend time, money, and resources on communications and materials that have little impact—and are left wondering why they don't work. They tend to blame the speech, ad, logo, brochure, email campaign, or website, and fail to see the most likely culprit: there is no strong concept for people to attach to.

Remember the "Think Small" and "Lemon" ads for Volkswagen under the supervision of William Bernbach? Multiple messages about Volkswagen were woven together under the concept of simplicity that contradicted the traditional association of automobiles with luxury. Each piece in the campaign built upon the other. And although these ads date back to the 1950s, they are still remembered and the concept remains clear.

Or consider the farewell speech given to cadets of the U.S. Military Academy by General Douglas MacArthur. His theme of "Duty, Honor, Country" was for the soldiers who would follow in his footsteps, reminding them of their purpose in becoming soldiers. The specific words in the talk may not be recalled, but the concept of service was forever etched in the hearts and minds of his audience.[2]

Whether you are communicating with internal or external audiences, your story should tap into what you want to inspire. This is how

you affect people's beliefs—which in turn drives their thoughts and actions, resulting in the positive outcomes you desire.

YOUR STORY

> The brands that win are the brands that tell a great story.
>
> —**Mitch Joel**, President, Mirum[3]

Why do we continue to talk about telling your "story"? What does this mean, and why are stories so important for communicating your Purpose?

Take a closer look at exactly why stories are good for business and how to begin telling yours.

Research by Harvard professors and developmental psychologists Robert Kegan and Howard Gradner shows that people are able to effect real change only when their emotions are engaged. And stories are the most powerful way of engaging people at an emotional level. Stories cause people to think, feel, and behave differently.[4] People remember and repeat stories.

Think of all the folklore that exists around the most powerful brands. Everyone has a story about Southwest Airlines, The Container Store, or Apple. Those stories help to perpetuate and reinforce these brands in the marketplace. These brands have reached the point where others tell their stories for them—sharing their experiences with the world. Now take a look at your own company and ask: who are the people telling your stories and what are they saying about you?

Stories support a complex concept—such as a corporate Purpose and all the values and behaviors that go with it—through narrative that makes these ideas more understandable and real. Embed Purpose into your culture by helping employees understand your *why* through stories that engage and empower them. Then you can begin to expand your stories to include stakeholders outside the company.

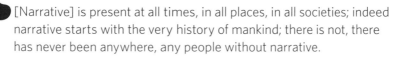

> [Narrative] is present at all times, in all places, in all societies; indeed narrative starts with the very history of mankind; there is not, there has never been anywhere, any people without narrative.
>
> —**Roland Barthes,** *An Introduction to the Structural Analysis of Narrative*[5]

Painting a picture through story connects your message at a deep, emotional level. You get to bypass stubborn logic by drawing people in. Remember, belief—not statistics—moves you through the sequence to advocacy and achieving your desired outcomes. But don't be concerned that your stories need to be long narratives or "once upon a time" tales. A great story can be as short as a few sentences.

Which do you find more compelling?

Our safety goals:
By complying with our safety rules and procedures, we can achieve our goal of zero recordable safety incidents.

OR

Our safety story:
Last week, one of our engineers stopped work when he saw his coworkers creating a dangerous work environment by ignoring one of our safety procedures. His intervention saved life and limb for one of his teammates. Protecting each other is what our safety rules and procedures are all about. Our goal is for every one of our people to go home safely at the end of the day, every day.

Stories help us remember the most important moments in our lives and allow us to share what we believe in and connect with. When your employees, clients, and partners inevitably talk about your company, you can help shape what they say by arming them with memorable brand stories.

And lest you think that stories are all light and fluffy, good stories can also add monetary value to your brand. For example, look at the experiment *New York Times* magazine columnist Rob Walker conducted.

Walker wrote stories to accompany random thrift store items posted for sale on eBay—and he saw something amazing happen. The value of those virtually worthless items rose 2,700 percent over the purchase price. A cracked ceramic horse, for instance, purchased for $1.29, sold for $46.

Nothing about the objects changed other than that they came with a story. The stories were not even real—they were fabricated for the experiment.[6]

If a random, simple story has the power to change even a worthless item into something coveted, imagine the impact purposeful stories can have on your brand. Stories have almost mythical properties—they are memorable, they promote understanding, they are repeatable, and they ultimately inspire action.

You have seen us using the story of Moguls, Inc. to help generate understanding of the ideas offered throughout this book.

In Appendix C, we have broken down in much more detail the three steps to help you start capturing, crafting, and communicating your stories.

Share your stories at every opportunity. Tell prospective employees about the ways your team acts in alignment with your Purpose. Brag on those who are getting it right. Make stories part of your folklore, inextricably tied to your brand. This is one of the best ways to help people come to know, believe in, and connect with your business.

YOUR IMAGE

So what happens if you come up with an absolutely brilliant and powerful concept and great narrative, but the execution falls short? The short answer is nothing. You waste your resources when you fail to design communications that have impact.

Let's face it—we do judge books by their covers. But the value of great design in telling your brand story is often underestimated. Design is what we see, and what we see, we understand. Well-designed communications materials reinforce your key points, strengthen connections, and build credibility for your story.

A picture is worth a thousand words, as they say, and a visual identity can communicate in a moment what it takes dozens of carefully crafted messages to say. When attempting to connect and communicate with people at an emotional level, imagery is one of the most effective tools in your arsenal. Consider carefully whether the creative strategy behind your brand image fits with your messages.

Take a close look at your current visual identity and consider what may need to be reevaluated to better match what you stand for. People respond to images before they read any words, so consider the aesthetics of your logo, literature, website, and all communications. What do they say about your brand? Do they reflect your personality and ideals? Do they support and work in harmony with your FOCUS?

Does the way you present your company visually tell the story of your Purpose? Is your creative strategy in line with the values you've claimed? How does the look and feel of your brand convey the experience of working with your company? This goes far beyond the application of your logo to all of your communications—it is verbal, visual, and experiential—from the way people answer the phone to the style of photography you use.

Consider your experience with an Apple product. There is great thought put into the design of every component—even the box that your new phone or laptop comes in. Every single piece has been considered carefully so that it adds to the experience, with nothing extraneous or inconsistent. Some of us even keep the Apple boxes because they are an important emotional part of the entire experience and too nice to toss.

The design of each element of communication, from logos to websites to collateral and packaging, must be pushed from merely functional to experiential. Exceptional design connects on a visceral level, engages people, and has the power to influence. Design ultimately helps to establish a brand that employees, potential employees, customers, suppliers, partners, and investors recognize and remember.

How does a favorite company logo or packaging make you feel? Do they provide a certain sense of expectation? Does just seeing a Nike logo or billboard make you want to engage in something physical? Does it make you think about the experiences that go with the products? Symbols and images, when used well, have the power to move us. In fact, many people who love Harley-Davidson are so attached to the brand that they tattoo the company's logo on their bodies.

> Great designers, like visionary business leaders, create value by exploring without limitation through the psyche and psychology of consumers. They assemble teams of individuals who see the world through different eyes and explore what should be as opposed to what is. They show discipline in doing more with less. By combining forces, we can create new business opportunities and the pathways to manifest consumer needs, emotions, and aspirations. By so doing, we generate revenue and sustainable growth for business.
>
> —**Ravi Sawhney and Deepa Prahalad**, *Business Week*[7]

Whether you have the in-house resources or you hire an external firm, be sure the design of your communications is compelling and differentiated. Your brand's image is well worth the investment.

And while it's important to ensure that those who create your materials have expert skills, it is equally important for them to understand and believe in your Purpose. Otherwise, your brand experiences may miss the mark.

YOUR RESOURCES

If you are truly passionate about the work you have done to this point, don't lose momentum by short-changing your communication efforts. There can be no half-measures. Create a budget that takes into account the necessary time, money, and resources for crafting and sharing your story. Be realistic. Great communications programs are a worthwhile investment. Doing things well the first time not only improves the effectiveness of your efforts, but it also saves you the time, cost, and pain of doing things over.

The capabilities of those entrusted with your brand communications directly impact the effectiveness of your efforts. When looking for a partner, search for branding, marketing, and design professionals who are not "yes people." Look for individuals or firms who can both guide and challenge you to effectively shape and share your brand story.

As with any of your suppliers or partners, make sure their values are aligned with yours and that they understand what you stand for. Push them to develop solutions that will help move you closer to your FOCUS.

> Being found is nice, but it's the experience and engagement that occurs (or not) that really matters. There are many ways to get eyeballs to your content, but what really matters is what happens when you get there.
>
> —**Mike Myatt,** *Forbes* contributor[8]

Assign a capable team to spearhead and manage the entire FUSE phase. Depending on your company, this can be a single senior-level employee, an internal marketing team, a trusted outside partner—or any combination of these.

This team or individual should have the belief, skills, and authority to set out clear expectations with regard to sharing your purposeful brand story. They should monitor all communications efforts closely to make sure everything FILTERs through your Purpose. Whoever manages these efforts needs to have unwavering support from the very top of the company. If too many people are involved in managing communications, or if there is no centralized control, the results can be chaotic and ineffective. Conversely, when a small group of experts directs all of your communications, the results have the greatest chance for making a lasting impact.

Once you have established strong core messages and connected your brand image through flawless execution, you are finally ready to start sharing your story.

Chapter 15

———

Share
Your Story

██

WHEN IT IS TIME TO START COMMUNICATING WHAT YOUR COMPANY BELIEVES, YOU WANT TO START WITH YOUR INTERNAL STAKEHOLDERS BEFORE RELEASING ANYTHING OUTSIDE YOUR WALLS. YOUR PURPOSE AND VALUES SHOULD RESONATE AND LIVE INSIDE YOUR COMPANY TO ENSURE THE EXPERIENCES OTHERS HAVE WITH YOUR BRAND MATCH WHAT YOU SAY AND DO. WE CALL THIS BUILDING YOUR BRAND FROM THE INSIDE OUT.

Your approach may vary depending on your size, complexity, geography, and budget. But regardless of these factors, it is best for your leadership to communicate from the inside out—first, with your management and employees, then with your external audiences.

Always start with *why* your company decided to undertake this initiative and then share how this will affect each group. People will evaluate what your story means to them and decide whether or not it is believable and rings true. Don't try to push everything into one message. It is helpful if you bring your stakeholders along in stages and avoid overwhelming them with too much detail at any one time.

Facts, stats, and figures do not have the ability to inspire as well as an emotional message does. Remember Martin Luther King's "I Have a Dream" speech and JFK's "Ask Not" Inaugural Address; the words they used to move masses needed no PowerPoint decks or graphs because they struck a deep emotional chord.

THE HUMAN FACTOR

Throughout the communication process, you are striving for widespread awareness, understanding, and alignment with your Purpose. Achieving this is dependent on not only sharing what you believe, but also connecting with what others believe. At this point, it is helpful to understand how the power of emotions, the power of groups, and the power of belief can make or break your best efforts.

> The mind can be convinced, but the heart must be won.
>
> —**Simon Sinek**, Twitter post[1]

The Power of Emotions

Remember that human beings are, by nature, emotional before they are rational. Emotions cause people to act; then rational thinking follows to either confirm or negate the action. Behavior is initially driven by emotion before it is validated through rationalization.

Facts do not have the power to change behaviors. Furthermore, many times they can't even change our minds once our emotions are entrenched. In 2005 and 2006, University of Michigan researchers conducted a series of studies, finding that when people who had previously read incorrect information in news stories were exposed to corrected facts, those facts did not change their minds. Many of them remained rooted even more strongly in their original beliefs. Legitimate facts simply were not powerful enough to battle misinformed, emotional beliefs.[2]

What this means for you as you share your company's story is that it absolutely has to be right the first time. People make decisions quickly and react to new messages immediately based on how they feel about what they see and hear. Any analytical facts and figures that follow a message can only help to either support or refute their initial feelings. Emotions trump facts every time.

In 2005, about a year *after* he was diagnosed with pancreatic cancer, Apple CEO Steve Jobs stood before the graduating class of Stanford University to tell three stories of his life about connecting the dots, love and loss, and death. Jobs' address is extremely moving and powerful, as it instills confidence in the form of reality paired with personal reflection. He concludes his speech with a quote that he once saw and remembered forever, which read, "Stay hungry. Stay foolish."

Steve Jobs was a visionary, creative genius, and revolutionary innovator who transformed the world and continues to inspire others even after his death.

As an inspirational leader, Jobs knew that the way to connect with his audience and have his messages remembered was to create an emotional connection. He did not show slides or use a computer. He simply spoke from his heart in a way that boosted and encouraged his audience to take action.

People want to follow those who inspire them and help them believe in themselves—not those who hammer away with lists and details. If you want others to hear, understand, and believe in your message, touch their emotions before your attempt to teach their brains.

The Power of Groups

Emotional engagement happens not only at the individual level, but also in groups. This dynamic of "collective thinking" is important for leaders to remember when attempting to encourage an entire company to move in the same direction.

One example of the power of appealing to a group is seen in the effective Texas litter campaign that dates back to the 1980s. Texas had a huge litter problem, and while highway signs were spread across the state asking citizens not to litter, they were having no impact. The state called in Sacramento-based Dan Syrek for help.

Research revealed that the biggest contributors to the litter problem were 18- to 24-year-old males who liked country music and drove pickup trucks. Syrek leveraged the emotions of that group for the campaign, featuring well-known Texas athletes and musicians in a series of upbeat TV spots. These ads, complete with country-rock music, showed the famous Texans picking up trash and throwing it away properly. Each spot ended with the simple line, "Don't mess with Texas."

The campaign tapped into the group identity of those target Texans, reshaping it to say that Texans don't litter. Littering is not part of who they are as a group.

Within a year, litter had declined 29 percent. During the first five years of the campaign, roadside litter decreased 72 percent, and the number of cans on the roadside dropped 81 percent. By 2010, research showed that 82 percent of Texans understood that "Don't mess with Texas" means "Don't litter."[3]

And what's amazing is that Texans so identified with and internalized the motto that, to outsiders, it became associated with the Texan "brand." Very few people outside of the state even knew it was an anti-litter campaign. It was just a part of Texan culture.

So as you're working to bring people along, try to tap into their group identity. Use emotional appeals to affect the group's behavior as a whole. People care about their group identity, they act on it, and they find power in it.

The Power of Belief

Think about your existing mission or vision statements and be honest. How many of your employees remember or recite them? How many employees act in accordance with them?

Fight the urge to tuck your newly uncovered Purpose, mission, vision, values, and behaviors away in an employee handbook or post them on your wall and consider your efforts complete.

If you want to engage your employees, you need to reach out to them in ways that help them believe your company can have a positive impact on their day-to-day lives. Help employees understand how they will benefit—individually and collectively. And in turn, through their efforts, your company can have a positive influence and profound impact on the world.

People want to know how a shift in focus away from the bottom line and toward a meaningful Purpose affects their livelihoods, their work, and their relationships with the company.

When shaping your story, start with your *why*. Begin with something people can have a gut, emotional reaction to before you attempt to support your message with facts and details.

For example, which of these is more compelling?

How we behave:
All customer service employees must now take a few minutes on each service call to engage in small talk and personal interest chatter with clients.

OR

What we believe:
Our customers are, first and foremost, people who deserve respect and warm interactions with us. We want them to feel that they are speaking to people who care about their issues every time they call. Whenever appropriate, employees should take an extra few minutes on each call to engage personally with clients.

This is a small example, but the point is clear: when employees understand *why* their behavior is expected to change, they are more willing to make adjustments. When their beliefs align with the beliefs you profess as a company, they are more inclined to engage in supporting behaviors.

And when people feel empowered to act in ways that align with their own beliefs, behaviors won't have to be prescribed by leadership; employees will move your company toward its Purpose in ways that are most authentic to them. This brings you one step closer to advocacy.

FROM THE INSIDE OUT

For optimum results, reveal your story from the inside out by using the following order: executive leadership, management teams, influencers, all employees, and outside audiences. This order is important. If you were to first communicate directly with your employees, your management would not be able to reinforce and support your messages or answer employee questions. By bringing people along in this manner, you will help your story travel in a lateral as well as a top-down fashion.

Executive Leadership

Executives serve as the primary models for middle management with regard to Purpose-based decision-making and actions. With the rest of the company looking to this group for guidance, your leaders need ongoing information and support.

Since company leaders were likely involved in shaping your message, many of your initial communications will be familiar to them. Their primary responsibility is to ensure that the FOCUS messages are communicated, supported, and modeled from the very top. They will carry the flag, continually providing information about what is expected of the entire company.

Management Teams

Your managers and supervisors interact with direct reports daily. They are the front line in ensuring that employees believe in and behave in alignment with your Purpose. It is this group who communicates the value of the changes and holds their teams accountable. They also serve as role models and advisors for employees below them. Their buy-in is critical.

There is a huge difference in the way managers share your messages when they see themselves as an important part of the change. You can build support and create inclusion by involving managers early.

When you address managers, acknowledge that this group plays an important role in this process—they are active participants, not just recipients of messaging from above. Engage them as partners and encourage them to add to the momentum your leadership team has started.

Training for this audience is done in two parts. First, answer their questions about what your FOCUS means for them and their jobs—remember, they too are employees. Reassure them they will have the support necessary for making any changes expected of them, and their involvement will be critical in shaping the future of the company. Whenever possible, be detailed and direct—the more real you can make the idea of Purpose for them, the less likely they are to disengage.

Second, give them materials that explain and reinforce the messages to their direct reports. Allow them to localize and customize these secondary messages to fit their area, function, region, or group to make them relevant to their team. Be sure they are equipped to tell all employees what is expected of them, what working purposefully will mean to them, why the company is moving in this direction, and how this will affect their daily lives. Empower these management leaders by arming them with training, talking points, information, and resources. They are the ones responsible once you have left the room.

Influencers

We all know that the traditional "cascading" communications model tends to fail as you get two or three levels into an organization. So how do you reach an entire organization effectively? Discovering how informal communications networks operate within your organization can greatly impact the success of your efforts.

> Did you know that just 3 percent of your company's employees could influence almost the entirety of your employee base? That's according to Innovisor, a company that specializes in Organizational Network Analysis (ONA).[4]

Influencers connect this "informal network" within your company, and they are the ones who others look to for advice, mentorship, opinions, and general know-how. They are not necessarily the ones *you* trust. They are the people employees trust. And they may or may not show up at the top of an organizational chart. These people have immense power to affect internal change initiatives—for good or ill.

Influencers are capable of moving fellow employees past negative reactions to change. They can bridge disconnected groups to support unity. They are crucial for your shift toward Purpose because they can help to spread ideas and emotions across divisions in a company, ensuring more uniform adoption.

Here's the problem: you probably have no idea who these people are.

"To this day, I have never come across a single CEO who knew who their most influential employees were when the number of employees exceeded one hundred," said Jeppe Vilstrup Hansgaard, CEO of Innovisor.

ONA (Organizational Network Analysis) researchers, such as Innovisor, use algorithms to create mathematical models of the most influential employees and the groups that they influence within an organization.

Novozymes, a Denmark-based leader in bio-innovation, employs more than 6,000 people in 30 countries. With a workforce of that scale, it's impossible for a leader to know who the most influential people are at any given location.

The company was launching a quality initiative at its China plant, and used Organizational Network Analysis to identify the right people to engage as compliance ambassadors. They were able to reach 82 percent of their employees through that core group of ambassadors. Instead of relying on top-down communications that might or might not have taken hold, they reached the majority of their people directly through the peers who were the most trusted for information.

Employees are between four and six times more influenced by their peers than by their managers. So when it comes time to share an important message or lead change, don't depend solely on traditional top-down communications methods—deliver messages straight to the most influential people in the company.

These influencers can be powerful allies and ambassadors when they believe in your Purpose and are convinced that the coming changes will be positive. In turn, their commitment fuels stronger engagement company wide.

Without over-formalizing this influencer group, equip them with the messages and tools they need to both reassure themselves and encourage others. Then empower them to tell the story in their own way. Allow them to take some ownership. The more authentic their voices are, the better. You don't want an entire group of influencers who sound like they're just parroting the boss. You also don't want them to become skeptical or derail the process.

Remember, this group can be just as strong an influence negatively as they can be positively. If people within your influencer group voice serious concerns, address them early. Show particular care with your influencers because where they go, your employee base will likely follow.

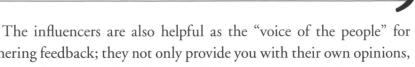

To persuade the undecided, send in someone they trust.

—Abraham Lincoln[5]

The influencers are also helpful as the "voice of the people" for gathering feedback; they not only provide you with their own opinions, but they also reveal where the rest of the company stands. In fact, this is perhaps their most critical role in any transformation.

All Employees

The next audience is your entire employee population. While executives set the vision and managers support you in getting there, it's the employees performing the work and interacting with customers who make your efforts either fly or fall—they are the ones who have to deliver.

Remember when presenting any new idea that first impressions are lasting. Use your initial communication to share what your Purpose means for the company and how employees should benefit. They will need time to process what is shared, just as your executive team needed time between the discovery sessions to absorb and reflect.

Building a purposeful brand requires long-term commitment, as this initiative can't be summed up in a simple email or memo; it will require discussions at each level and branch of the company explaining how Purpose is intended to have a positive impact on both performance and profits.

In addition to managers and influencers, another group you need to pay special attention to at this stage of communications is the fence sitters.

The fence sitters are employees who are neither enthusiastic about the proposed change nor fiercely against it. They are uncertain because they can't see the value for the company, or they worry about the impact on their own work, or they are not convinced that the company will fully commit and follow through.

We are not aware of any mathematical algorithm for identifying these people. As you roll out your initial communications, use feedback forms, internal interviews, and insight from influencers to identify this group. *The Fence Sitter Identification* exercise shares some characteristics that may be helpful in determining who is on the fence about your FOCUS.

Once identified, it's important to reach out to these people with conversation and support. Connect them with the influencers who are best equipped to reach them. Fence sitters should not be ignored because they can serve as the tipping point for any effort. They can be found at all levels of your organization, and winning them over may mean the difference between success and failure.

With all internal groups, be sure to communicate these points:

- ● Why you are pursuing this undertaking.

- ● Why you believe it is important for everyone.

- ● How your FOCUS will impact the company's future.

- ● How you plan to infuse your culture with Purpose.

- ● The role employees will play in making these efforts successful.

When communicating with employees, deliver your story in a clear and compelling manner. Let them see your passion. They will become more engaged when they witness how committed you are to your company's Purpose. And to achieve maximum impact, consider making your presentation interactive.

Ralph Vasami, CEO of Universal Weather & Aviation, Inc., is a few years into his company's Purpose journey. He has discovered the best way to foster understanding of his messages is to "lead, not tell." Vasami brings his people along with interactive presentations that get them engaged in the story. He asks leading questions that foster conversation and dialogue in the middle of his presentation. He welcomes questions and encourages his audience to "get it." This process allows Vasami to gain valuable feedback in real time and confirm that his message is understood.

End each communication by asking for comments, questions, and feedback. Every dialogue will prove useful in helping you refine your story, identify potential red flags, and prioritize actions. Make sure to emphasize that you value their thoughts and input and you are counting on their engagement to build your purposeful brand.

After sharing your FOCUS within your company, don't be surprised if you witness some frustration. Change is challenging. Employees might think you are forcing them to believe and act in ways they don't yet understand. In short order, you will discover which employees are interested in getting behind and supporting your efforts.

Keep in mind you cannot rely on one broad, sweeping announcement. You will need to repeat your story often and continue to reinforce your *why* again and again to nurture advocacy.

External Audiences

When it's time to start sharing your story externally, it is important to connect your truths with the full brand experience all stakeholders have with your company through every image, message, and interaction.

Your Purpose should influence how each stakeholder experiences and perceives your brand—from your voice mail greetings, your business cards, your website, your office décor, your product offerings, to your advertising messages, and everything in between. Communicating and demonstrating what you stand for to your external audiences enhances the rapport they develop with your business.

If you are ever in Houston, Texas, we recommend that you sign up for one of the tours through the corporate offices of Blinds.com. From the moment you step off the elevators, you know you are in a special place. While you might expect a place that takes online orders for window coverings to be boring and one dimensional, it is quite the opposite. There is life, energy, and excitement in every square foot. Perhaps one of the most interesting parts of the tour is when they walk you through a replica of the alley in which the company started—complete with brick walls and rubber rats in the windows. It reminds them of how far they have come and keeps them connected to *why* the company was started. At each stage along the tour you feel the company's culture and experience an entire group of employees working toward a common Purpose—"To help people become better than they ever believed possible." It is both powerful and memorable.

Sharing your story externally is about more than just revealing what you stand for. Your company's Purpose and values provide a foundation—a jumping-off point for all efforts to enhance your brand and build strong relationships. Sharing your story should feel authentic and natural, never forced. When done well, these communications help develop trust and loyalty between your brand and your external audiences.

UPS' famous "What can Brown do for you?" campaign was successful because it recognized that for most people, their only experience with the UPS brand came through interactions with the driver and the quality of their package delivery. Along with the well-known marketing slogan, UPS worked to create a very consistent experience for people receiving packages—from the appearance of the drivers and their trucks to the speed and quality of the service.[6]

Building external awareness is an ongoing process. This is not a campaign with a beginning and an end, but a journey. Stay the course. Keep true to your company's story in a way that demonstrates great thought and ongoing commitment to your Purpose.

Your messages here will differ somewhat from what is released internally, but there should still be strong consistency and transparency as your communications are created with each audience in mind. Meet with your outside stakeholders to learn what messages resonate with them. Bring these groups along in a way that connects them with your beliefs.

To build trust and advocacy, follow through on what you promise. Clients, suppliers, partners, and communities are more likely to be interested in what you say if it rings true with them and their experiences match your rhetoric.

> Sharing your Purpose is not an initiative or a campaign; it's a journey.

As we pointed out, all your communications should start from the inside and move outward. By engaging your employees in the proper sequence, and articulating what makes your company great, they then help influence all your other stakeholders. You are giving these groups powerful reasons to form long-term allegiance with your brand.

When people become engaged and committed to your cause, they begin to tell your stories. And when your stakeholders become your advocates, find ways to either acknowledge or reach out to them. These people are your "tribe," and their loyalty will dramatically impact the long-term success of your brand.

Savage Thinking in Action

PLANNING THE STORY OF PURPOSE

Moguls, Inc. reached the FUSE phase with a sense of relief at finally being able to craft the platform for messaging. Change hardly feels real while it's restricted to talk exchanged between a small team, even when that team is committed to making things happen. They were excited and more than ready to tell Mogul's story of Purpose to the company.

The starting point was developing an internal platform for unveiling the company's new FOCUS. Ralph and Alex—who shared internal communications responsibilities—brainstormed with Anne to craft their initial messages.

"There are three things you absolutely have to get across," Anne told them. "First, you have to tell them why management went on this journey in the first place. That's going to be a big question. Second, you have to make very clear what benefits the company is going to experience—and what the benefits are for each employee. Let them know that this isn't about making their life harder; it's going to improve things for everyone. Finally, you have to explain why they should care. Help them believe in what you're talking about here."

John hovered in these meetings, following up frequently with emails and calls about their progress. It was critical that these messages be right. He and the rest of the team knew the way they exposed the information in the first wave of communications would influence how well their Purpose was received—there was no second chance at the first impression.

As they began creating their messaging guidelines, Moguls' executives learned about Organizational Network Analysis (ONA). Campbell challenged the additional external cost, but John pointed to the research to justify the expense. "This won't just help us identify our key influencers in the company; it's also going to help us deliver these messages in a way that improves understanding and, hopefully, belief. We know how important it is to ensure our people believe."

"Plus," he continued, "once we know who these influencers are, they can keep an ear to the ground and give us a heads-up if there's something bubbling up from the other employees that could be a problem. We're going to need feedback if this rollout is going to be a success, and I don't know how effective we are at gathering that now."

When the ONA survey analysis was delivered, the leaders were surprised. None of the company's identified influencers were the people the executives had supposed them to be. John was astounded by the difference between the list of influential employees he'd had in his head and the list that the research delivered to him.

Allison was on the list, and John saw it as more evidence of his growing belief that she was the right person to succeed him.

He put his trust in the information, asking his internal communications team to use the list of names provided as their go-to influencers, the best informal vehicle for the flow of communication.

Anne reminded the team that it was important for the influencers to support Mogul, Inc.'s FOCUS with their own words—providing a measure of authenticity to the messages and delivering the peer-to-peer communication that was simply unachievable through top-down channels. If they were seen as ventriloquists' dummies, simply reiterating corporate-speak, they wouldn't be effective.

As the rollout progressed, even Campbell had to acknowledge the value of the influencers; they became an invaluable resource in helping management take the pulse of their culture.

PLANTING INTERNAL SEEDS OF CHANGE

Armed with the knowledge that their people would need to believe in something before they would think or act differently, Moguls' executives created a schedule for a roadshow where John could get in front of employees and share the company's new statements—their Purpose, mission, vision, values, and behaviors—in his charismatic, genuine way. He asked Allison to accompany him, both because of her influencer status and because he wanted his people to see her infectious enthusiasm for Purpose.

They visited Moguls' five offices in person. At each location, they held a 30-minute interactive presentation that took employees on the journey the executives had experienced over the previous several months. For John, it was a bit of an emotional roller coaster, reliving the ups and downs, and the hard choices they'd made.

He then gave tangible reasons to believe in the direction the company was taking, and answered questions from the assembled employees.

Most of the employees had a strong, positive reaction to the messages; John's and Allison's presentations were largely met with applause, congratulations, and support. John heard a dozen variations of, "Wow, this is great!"

Allison and John compared notes on their favorite comments after the fact. Allison's was, "This is going to bring the company together in a really great way."

John's favorite was, "I am glad to be part of a company that cares enough to commit to this journey."

But there were a few at every town hall that sat silently with furrowed brows. At each presentation, one or two would speak up to say, "Why are we doing this? We're fine just the way we are." Sometimes, these dissenters brought up previous attempts at change, suggesting that this process was just another "flavor-of-the-month" management idea.

John listened empathetically to each comment, but let every group know that this process was different. "Purpose is going to influence our culture in a positive way. Every decision we make from now on is going to be affected by Purpose," he said. "This is not a fad. It's a new way of living for Moguls—one that acknowledges the successes of the company's past and provides a roadmap for an even greater future."

He quoted stats about how well companies who operated based on Purpose perform financially, and showed employees how often these Purposeful brands ended up on "best places to work" lists. He let his people know that this process was about making each of their jobs more meaningful and rewarding.

The CEO acknowledged that the transition would not be easy, but he insisted that the entire management team was committed to making it work. "I'm asking for your trust, your patience, and your support," he said.

Following the road show, the company buzzed with chatter. Small talk in the hallways and break rooms expressed people's optimism about the positive endeavor, as well as many questions and scattered concerns.

As communications began to flow internally, weekly emails gave employees information about the progress of the initiative and shared successes. Gradually, a collective sense emerged that knowing and understanding their FOCUS was beginning to help employees work better together, and new ideas were flowing like an uncapped fire hydrant.

SHARING THE STORY EXTERNALLY

Once they felt they were organized and credibly living their Purpose internally, the executive team agreed it was time to draft an external communications plan.

As Moguls' leaders considered the wants and needs of each group of stakeholders, Anne gave them three questions to contemplate: Why would anyone outside our company care about our Purpose? What does our FOCUS mean to external stakeholders? And how do purposeful experiences benefit people outside our company's walls?

They created the first drafts of their company stories and wove them into the website, emails, proposals, and other communication vehicles, both inside and outside the company.

For a few days after the external launch, it seemed like they would see no response. Then, in surprising numbers, the executives began to receive notes from clients expressing their support for the company's Purpose and rewarding them for their efforts. The warm, enthusiastic reactions were a welcome and unexpected bonus that re-energized the team.

The results over the next several months were enough to make every member of the leadership team happy. They began to win business in areas that had previously eluded them as their name spread to new geographies and new industries. Fresh conversations were happening, and they realized the executives that were seeking them out now, the ones with whom they were building relationships, were better clients who more strongly aligned with their Purpose.

They knew then that they were on the right track.

Chapter 16

Live
Your Story

‎

**LET'S FACE IT; BUILDING AND MORPHING A CULTURE IS NO EASY TASK.
THE BEST LAID PLANS IN THE FILTER PHASE CAN STILL GO AWRY WHEN
YOU ARE DEALING WITH THE COMPLEXITIES OF BLENDING HUMAN
BEHAVIOR AND COMPANY OPERATIONS.**

This part of FUSE is about aligning your words and actions inside
and outside the walls of your company. Just because you've shared it
doesn't mean you are living it. You must influence all stakeholder experiences by making your FOCUS an inextricable part of your company's
DNA. You do this by leading with Purpose, nurturing employee relationships, and strengthening external connections.

People tend to resist and push back when asked to modify their ideas
or behaviors. This is just human nature. But don't let this sidetrack your
efforts. Change is good, it's even essential; however a cultural transformation can take years. Refuse to let existing habits, beliefs, and territorial
issues become roadblocks to becoming a purposeful brand.

> As your culture begins to shift, there are several traps you can easily fall into that can limit your success and derail your Purpose. Take a look at the *Culture Traps* in Appendix A.

In this chapter we share the importance of leading your company's efforts from the very top of the organization.

WALK THE TALK

Purposeful brands start with great leadership. No matter what you ask of your employees, if your leadership team is not passionate and they are not modeling your desired language and behaviors, your people will sense a lack of commitment and begin to disconnect. Any cultural shift is destined to fail without belief and consistency from the top of the organization.

Strive to be the best example of the kind of behavior you wish to see in others. A leader who exemplifies this admirable trait is Herb Kelleher, co-founder of Southwest Airlines.

> We had the privilege of flying from Houston to Dallas with Mr. Kelleher in 2014. Well, actually, we stood beside him in the boarding line.
>
> You see, he doesn't go to the front of the line. He boards between A and B sections. We spotted him at the gate check-in area and noticed crowds of people gathered around waiting to visit with him, shake his hand, or take a photo with him.
>
> This man who helped found one of the most envied airlines in the world had no air of importance or entitlement. He was friendly and open. He greeted each person as if he or she were family.

> We struck up a conversation with him about one of our favorite com-
> panies of all time—his. He didn't disagree, and was quick to tell us,
> "It's not about the money. I have told my employees every day that
> it is never about the money. It is about experiences and sharing time
> with others. It's about helping people take vacations, visit family, and
> get business done. I started this airline with the purpose of making
> it easier for people to fly, and this remains true—three decades later."
>
> As we boarded the plane, we were interested to see that he quietly
> made his way to the very back and took a seat in the last row. Half-
> way through the flight, he came whistling down the aisle with several
> drink orders. He served the drinks, chatted with the customers, and
> whistled back to the rear of the plane. As he passed our row, we
> gave him a thumbs-up and smiled.
>
> On one of his passes, he stopped by our row, bent down, and whis-
> pered, "You know, the last time I did this, one of the passengers told
> me I was the ugliest flight attendant he had ever seen and muttered
> something about the standards of the airline having slipped!" Need-
> less to say, he kept us in stitches throughout the flight.
>
> Before we landed, one of the flight attendants made a brief
> announcement about our honored guest aboard the flight. This
> brought smiles and lots of chatter when people finally realized who
> he was. But the most impressive part of our time with Mr. Kelleher
> was the fact that every airline employee he encountered, both on
> the plane and in each terminal, wanted to give him a hug and share
> a story with him. It was a pure demonstration of how to walk your
> talk and live your Purpose.

By demonstrating his own commitment to the values upon which the company was founded, Herb Kelleher created a culture where employees believe just as strongly in their airline's Purpose—"To democratize the skies."[1] He serves as a shining beacon for his people as well as for other corporate leaders who seek to inspire.

In the same vein, leaders that model "anti-behavior" show that these actions are acceptable. As Chris Jones, President of Swagelok Southeast Texas says, "You are what you tolerate."

The culture shift that makes a Purpose initiative successful starts with your company's leadership team. The only way to guide an entire company away from the bottom line and toward something of meaning is to have resolute engagement and trust at the top. If employees don't believe in or trust their leaders, they won't feel obliged to adopt any new language and behaviors. By committing to modeling your ideal behaviors and shaping your leadership style to align with your FOCUS, you can begin to shift your company in the right direction.

> Great organizations don't just drive profits, they lead people, and they change the course of industries and sometimes our lives in the process.
>
> —**Simon Sinek**, *Start with Why*[2]

In *Firms of Endearment,* the authors reference this leadership attitude by saying, "FoE leaders facilitate, encourage, reward, recognize and celebrate their employees for being of service to their communities and the world at large, for no reason other than it is the right thing to do."[3]

APPOINT A CPO

One way to keep your Purpose efforts on track is to appoint a member of your leadership team to oversee this work. You need a dependable, reliable executive sponsor to ensure you remain vigilant in pursuit of your intended outcomes.

For some companies, we recommend appointing a Chief Purpose Officer (CPO) to fill this role—someone whose primary responsibility is encouraging and guiding the company's commitment to this work. While other C-suite executives are most concerned with those responsibilities that fall within their silos, the CPO is a cross-disciplinary leader who looks at the big picture and constantly assesses the company's performance. This person serves as the litmus test for any new initiative or major company effort by continually posing the question, "How will this action help us serve our Purpose?" This keeps people from chasing red herrings.

However, keep this in mind: while a CPO or other C-suite appointee can be highly effective in ensuring the success of your Purpose initiative, this person in no way replaces the responsibility of the CEO and other executive leaders to model your values and behaviors. You need everyone rowing in the same direction to match all experiences with your story.

Take a look at how these leadership qualities can be used in building a purposeful brand.

ENCOURAGE PROGRESS

Daniel Pink, in his book *Drive*, describes how people who make progress every day toward something they care about are more satisfied and fulfilled. Research shows that of all the things that can boost emotions, motivations, and perceptions during a workday, the single most important is making progress in purposeful work. And the more frequently people experience a sense of progress, the more likely they are to be productive in the long run. Whether they are trying to solve a major scientific mystery or simply produce a high-quality product or service, everyday progress—even a small win—can make all the difference in how they feel and perform.[4]

People gain more satisfaction from the accomplishment of a goal than from a monetary reward. When rewards are offered, that incentive eventually becomes the only motivator—and sometimes becomes an entitlement. When this happens, the intrinsic value of the accomplishment is lost.

SUPPORT FAILURE

Jay Steinfeld, CEO of Blinds.com, encourages failure. The company's "First Law of Marketing" and one of its core values is "Experiment without Fear of Failure." To demonstrate this commitment, Steinfeld set up two large, transparent tubes in his corporate office: one representing failed experiments, and the other successful ideas. Employees add a marble to one tube or the other each time an idea is tested—and yes, the "failed" tube has about one-third more marbles. Steinfeld is proud of that fact because he's seen the magnitude of the great ideas that have been successful. Not only are those ideas furthering his business, but his people have become even more motivated to try new things and explore new ideas without negative consequences.

This example demonstrates the importance of using failure as part of the learning process. Inspire people to reach their full potential by creating an environment where individuals are encouraged to reach for new levels of expertise without the fear that a failure might cost them their job. Give your employees the power to make decisions on their own and to learn from their choices. Foster a workplace where ideas are honored, growth is accelerated, and exciting discoveries unfold every day.

> I have not failed. I've just found 10,000 ways that won't work.
>
> —Thomas Edison[5]

EMPOWER OTHERS

What does it look like when leadership creates a culture in which their actions match their words? Ken Iverson of Nucor Steel shares an illuminating story about an incident that happened in 2006 demonstrating what can happen when employees are empowered by their leaders.

One mid-afternoon in March, the electricians at Nucor Steel received a call telling them that the electrical grid had failed at one of their plants. For a company that is dependent on electricity to melt the scrap metal that they forge into steel, this presented a crisis.

Three workers from two different states dropped what they were doing and traveled for several hours to get to the troubled facility as quickly as they could.

On the surface, this may not sound remarkable. But no supervisor or manager told them to go. There was no financial incentive for anyone in this trio. And the fact that they went so quickly to address the problem did not raise an eyebrow within the company.

You see, this is typical behavior at Nucor Steel. These three men knew that the company's productivity was on the line and took it upon themselves to correct the problem. There was no fanfare or expectation of special recognition—it was just a part of their culture to do what they could to support each other's success.

When you create a culture that allows employees to use their own judgment to help determine what is best for the company, you can expect to have great employees like these who believe that acting this way is just part of their jobs.

Is it any wonder that Nucor Steel returned 387 percent to stockholders in the five-year period surrounding this story?[6]

> "Seventy percent culture and 30 percent technology. The truth is, I'm not sure if it's 80 to 20 or 60 to 40 percent, but I'm certain our culture accounts for more than half of our success as a business.
>
> —**Ken Iverson**, Chairman and former CEO of Nucor Steel[7]

EMBRACE ALL STAKEHOLDERS

Internal Relationships

Engaging your people is essential to developing the kind of culture that supports your Purpose. This is a never-ending process that continues for the life of your company. It begins when you share your FOCUS with current employees, solicit their feedback, and encourage their support.

But as you move forward, you have the larger task of refining the ways in which you interact with your people at every level, continuing to infuse each touchpoint with Purpose. This starts by examining how you search for the right employees, onboard them, train them, and retain the best—those invested in helping you live your story.

> For employees, culture trumps everything else in your company—raises, location, offices, etc.—as long as their basic needs are being met. Culture is the most crucial factor in most employees' decisions to join, stay with, and advocate for a company. And they are looking to company leaders to set the tone.

Recruit on Purpose

Orient your recruitment efforts around hiring and keeping employees who embody the right values and are motivated by your FOCUS. When searching for these people, don't settle for solely reviewing CVs and past experience. The mindset you are seeking will most likely never show up on a resume. To find your purposeful employees you will need to take the time to ask deep questions about values and try to understand how an applicant might match with your ideals. You don't want to invest in people who will conflict with your culture—they won't be happy and neither will you.

Here are a few values-based recruiting questions:

Q What would you be doing if money was no obstacle?

◎ What types of activities make you feel energized and productive?

◎ What kinds of conversations stimulate your mind?

◎ How would you describe the ideal workplace?

◎ Can you tell me about your favorite accomplishment?

So what does purposeful hiring look like in today's business world? Look at how Google describes their recommended values-based recruiting questions for hiring their next "Nooglers."

> We're looking for our next Noogler—someone who's good for the role, good for Google and good at lots of things.
>
> Things move quickly around here. At Internet speed. That means we have to be nimble, both in how we work and how we hire. We look for people who are great at lots of things, love big challenges, and welcome big changes. We can't have too many specialists in just one particular area. We're looking for people who are good for Google—and not just for right now, but for the long term.
>
> This is the core of how we hire. Our process is pretty basic; the path to getting hired usually involves a first conversation with a recruiter, a phone interview, and an onsite interview at one of our offices. But there are a few things we've baked in along the way that make getting hired at Google a little different.
>
> We're looking for smart, team-oriented people who can get things done. When you interview at Google, you'll likely interview with four or five Googlers. They're looking for four things: leadership, role-related knowledge, how you think, and Googleyness.[8]

Google makes it clear from the start that their culture plays a heavy role in their hiring process, and that they're looking for people who align with their beliefs. If you think attempting to measure new job applicants against your Purpose seems daunting, take comfort in knowing that at least you won't have to sift through Google's tens of thousands of job applications received weekly.[9]

Another great purposeful hiring story comes from Zappos, an online shoe and clothing retailer. About a week into their intensive new employee training, they make every single new hire an offer: a few thousand in cash—plus full salary for the amount of time they've been in training—if they will quit and walk out the door right then.

Their rationale is if any new trainees are not in sync with the beliefs that drive the company, Zappos would rather not have them. If they can be tempted away by the money, they are not a good fit for the company's culture, and it's better for those new hires and for the business if they leave before any more is invested in them.[10]

It's a powerful statement to make to new hires: we believe so strongly in our Purpose and our company that we're willing to let go of people we spent weeks courting and recruiting rather than endanger the success of our culture.

Onboard on Purpose

To hire in alignment with your FOCUS, you must set clear expectations with new employees of what to anticipate when they come on board. Think about what you're "selling" in your recruiting process. What kind of impression do you make on people between the time of hire and when they start their jobs? What do new employees experience their first day of work—or the first 30 days? Is it aligned with the information they received during recruitment and initial training?

If it isn't, the disconnect is going to be a rude awakening for your new hires—and disillusioned employees might not stick around to see whether their experience will improve.

Most of us, when asked to identify our personal Purpose in life, look back with a blank stare. This is not a question generally heard. We spend little time identifying the right personal or career path but spend most of our time just getting on with life and going through the motions. Encourage your co-workers and employees to try the Personal Purpose exercises in Appendix B: *Finding Your Own Way*. The questions posed are designed to help people identify if they are in the right industry, best position and correct culture for fulfilling their own personal Purpose. Most who do this work are surprised and gratified with what they uncover.

Develop on Purpose

Often employers are quick to train on skills, process, and safety, but what about brand, Purpose, mission, vision, values, and behaviors? Each employee needs to begin the journey from awareness to advocacy from the first day on the job. What happens in the first month of employment has a huge impact on an employee's productivity and longevity with the organization. How well your company articulates your FOCUS and how quickly you build a deep connection with employees influences both their engagement and their job satisfaction.

The Container Store is an exemplary company that empowers its employees to deliver daily on the organization's Seven Foundation Principles.™ They understand how important training is for enhancing customer experiences and promoting employee and customer loyalty. Kip Tindell, chairman and CEO, made a powerful commitment with their robust employee training program.

"We are extraordinarily dedicated to finding and connecting with great talent. And after we hire GREAT employees, we focus on their training and development. The Container Store offers more than 263 hours of formal training for full-time employees in their first year with us—compared to the industry average of about eight hours. Another of our Seven Foundation Principles™ is, 'Intuition doesn't come to an unprepared mind; you must train before it happens.' Our commitment to providing our salespeople with everything they need to be successful in their careers provides value to employees and customers."[11]

Of course, development shouldn't stop once employees are on board and settled into their jobs. It's an ongoing part of a purposeful brand. In addition to the quality, safety, and technical training that should already be part of your business, consider creating robust

programs that instill and reinforce the collective behaviors you want, keeping them top-of-mind—to ensure you are aligning all words and actions.

While the number of hours committed to training programs is important, it's the quality and substance of these programs that really counts. Be sure all content supports what your company believes and that your expected behaviors are well defined and achievable. Give examples and share stories to make the information easy to retain and apply. Continue to share your *why* and make all training personally relevant.

Check out the *Outside-the-Classroom Training* exercise for some ideas on creative and engaging training.

> **Q** "What if we train our people and they leave?"
>
> **Q** "What if we don't train them and they stay?"

Retain on Purpose

Now that you've hired the best and trained them well, you want to hold onto them. They are instrumental in building brand advocacy.

People stay in jobs where they feel fulfilled, supported, and recognized. They want a voice. Search for ways to encourage feedback and then listen well. You will not only earn respect for being open, but also gain powerful insights.

Continual and consistent communication is key. In addition to formal, planned messages, find teachable moments in day-to-day situations. Help your managers identify golden opportunities to strengthen understanding of your Purpose and build positive connections between employees and your brand.

Many companies view culture as a major differentiator and a vital part of what they are selling. If this is the case, employee fit and cultural development are paramount.

Consider periodically gathering in small groups to brainstorm ways to better live your story. You may need to shake up your traditional teams by providing people opportunities to interact with peers whose backgrounds, skills, and experience differ from their own. When people are presented with challenges and opposing perspectives, they have an opportunity to stretch and grow as individuals.

As mentioned earlier, emotions trump reason. All the charts, graphs, and numbers in the world are powerless if they are not connected with an understanding of *why*. Encourage conversations about what your company believes and how each person's efforts are important. Your employees are interested in finding deeper meaning in their jobs and knowing how their efforts add value. Help them see that sharing a collective Purpose is more gratifying than achieving an individual goal. If your employees don't find a common point of connection with your company, they will resort to just getting by or marking time until something better comes along.

Working side by side with employees on the road to advocacy is challenging and takes vigilance. Keep your eyes clearly fixed on your vision and inspire others to stay on the right path.

When you experience the joy of associating with like-minded individuals and groups you will be forever changed—for the better. This will empower you to push for more purposeful connections, help employees be happier and more fulfilled, which ultimately benefits your bottom line.

External Relationships

While it may be tough to shape your internal culture, building lasting connections with your external stakeholders can prove even more challenging. Still, it is essential for moving you toward your vision. From customers, to partners, to investors, to communities; how you interact with those outside your company walls determines your ultimate success.

Do you hold your clients and suppliers to the same standards and behaviors expected of your employees? If not, consider whether these are the right partners for you. Take a close look at who you do business with and consider whether their values align with yours. Determine if you are making the right decisions regarding the customers you serve and partnerships you depend on. These are the people and businesses that can help you deliver on your Purpose.

Let your FOCUS and your FILTER help you to choose wisely, because those who you agree to associate with can either help you move closer to your vision or derail your efforts.

We've all been disappointed consumers before—when we believed in what we were being told and then our experience was a complete let down. This failure to connect erodes trust and diminishes reputations. But when what your company does lines up with what you say, you build loyalty.

Check to see if your words and actions match. Take time to scrutinize how people interact with your company. Examine every major touchpoint external stakeholders have with your business and challenge whether or not you're living your story authentically. Ask yourself if you would want to be a client of your company. Consider whether what you are promising is what they are experiencing.

Develop materials to help introduce your company to opportunities and follow through by making sure the experience of working with you aligns with what you communicate. Let customers discover what it is like to align with a purposeful brand and give them reasons to not only remain a customer, but also grow their relationship with you. Tell them what you believe in and how they fit in to your story.

> At the end of the day people won't remember what you said or did, they will remember how you made them feel.
>
> —Maya Angelou[12]

While working with a client who has locations in several different cities, we noticed that each office had a different way of answering the phone. This created an experience that varied from location to location.

When we mentioned this to leadership, they quickly implemented phone training for all their full-time and front desk relief employees. Now every caller has the same experience, no matter which office they're calling. It's a good example of a small detail that can have an impact on a client's experience and connection to the brand.

Don't get discouraged if all your efforts do not produce immediate results. Living your story is much like watching your children grow— you don't see them change every day, but when you look at a snapshot from a year ago you notice dramatic differences. Although becoming a purposeful company takes time, patience, and tenacity, much like parenting, the rewards are gratifying.

As mentioned earlier, The Container Store has a very robust and close-knit culture. In Chairman and CEO Kip Tindell's book, *Uncontainable: How Passion, Commitment, and Conscious Capitalism Built a Business Where Everyone Thrives*, he shares how they have built this culture with Seven Foundation Principles.™ But even this retail icon, with a strong Purpose and enviable culture, faces stiff challenges and stumbles along the way.

The Container Store went public in 2013. But since their initial offering the company has posted weak sales—making people wonder if a company that works hard at benefiting all stakeholders could keep its shareholders happy.

"It's been wonderful and terrible and good and bad," Tindell says about leading a public company. "It's a little more emotional than I thought it would be. It's like they're talking about your daughter. For the first time in my life, I have people saying, 'I don't like this.' If we were private, it would be fun to work on getting sales up. It's less fun because investors want you to do it in one quarter."

During this difficult time, Tindell turned to Jim Sinegal, the co-founder of Costco, for advice in managing expectations and this situation. Sinegal told him to keep the faith. He reminded Tindell that it takes time to find your "right" shareholders—the ones who want to be with you for the long haul. You have to prove you are a good long-term partner and resist worrying about the company's stock prices for the first 10 years.

"I am a little surprised that human beings can be so impatient," Tindell says. "If you retrieve your lure too fast you'll never catch any fish. It's stunning how slow you have to go. If you think you're fishing slowly enough, fish half again slower, and you'll catch many more."[13]

This one story reinforces the fact that becoming a purposeful brand is a marathon, not a sprint. Even when you are moving along the right path you will face new challenges and curve balls. You are in this for the long haul. That means staying true to what you believe, attracting others who trust in what you stand for, and keeping your eye on the ball. It is a formula that takes patience and tenacity—but the dividends are well worth the effort.

Expand on Purpose

Happy clients are your best source for continued business. But how often do you think through the ways in which you follow up with your customers and clients to keep them coming back? More often than not, we tend to send a bill and wait for them to call on us again. Search for the opportunities to expand the relationship, continue the conversation, and leave no room for competitors. Once a customer believes in your Purpose and then realizes how the employees in your company "walk your talk," they are more inclined to stay with you and be committed to your success. Then they will want to share their positive interactions with others and begin telling your stories.

Consider how you ask for referrals and collect stories to use in your marketing. These third-party endorsements are worth their weight in gold. This is the point when external stakeholders start to become your advocates by sharing your lore and inviting others to experience working with, for, and beside you. Ultimately, they will start to tell your story for you!

Living your story takes respecting the interconnectivity of all stakeholders and understanding how people move from awareness to advocacy. Building and maintaining a purposeful brand is a constant endeavor, and needs strong leaders shepherding it in the right direction at all times.

Everything runs more smoothly with a strong, cohesive culture: execution improves, efficiencies increase, employees are more engaged, customers are more satisfied, performance levels rise, and a company is more stable overall. It has even been argued that culture is the last remaining competitive advantage. When your organization nurtures all stakeholders to believe in *why* your business exists and where it is headed, you literally become unstoppable. This is how to build your purposeful brand.

YOU ARE HERE

▽ ① FOCUS: WHERE PURPOSE IS UNCOVERED

▽ ② FILTER: WHERE PURPOSE TAKES SHAPE

▼ ③ FUSE: WHERE PURPOSE COMES TO LIFE

When spider webs unite, they can tie up a lion.

—Ethiopian proverb

Savage Thinking in Action

A PURPOSEFUL CULTURE
SUPPORTS A PURPOSEFUL BRAND

John was grateful that Alex was fully on board with the Savage Thinking process now, because a huge part of the FUSE phase fell on her shoulders as the VP of HR.

Her first order of business—in accordance with their new Purpose Roadmap—was to reshape their recruiting of new employees to be in alignment with Moguls' FOCUS. Alex trained her HR representatives to look at more than an applicant's resume, asking questions about what drove them and whether they would be a cultural fit for the company, in addition to having the skills to do the job well.

As a result, Moguls, Inc. began to attract better applicants.

Alex burst into John's office one afternoon, grinning hugely. "Word on the street is spreading—Moguls cares about the legacy we're leaving and we care about the people who work to make it a reality. People want to work with us!"

The company also set new guidelines for onboarding and training employees. Their culture began to shift as new employees were brought into the business for their beliefs and not merely their skills and experience. The hallways were energized, and people were smiling.

Alex and her team put many new projects in place to reinforce their culture: behaviors cards, which allowed employees to recognize each other for living in accordance with their FOCUS; Purpose brainstorms, in which employees discussed areas where they could more efficiently and effectively deliver on their Purpose; a living wall where employees shared inspirations and examples of work that was meaningful to them.

The atmosphere within Moguls, Inc. was one of hope and anticipation. The employees believed they were part of something much bigger than themselves. They were committed to making a difference in the world and inspiring visionary leaders to unleash their talents.

Not all was sunshine and rainbows. Several employees self-edited, removing themselves from the company because they were used to the old way of doing things and were not interested in change. It also became evident to management that some employees would never elect to leave, nor would they ever understand the new direction the company had taken, so they were let go.

It was after a small wave of personnel adjustments that John had a crisis of faith. The economy had taken a dip, and the leaders were back to chasing any potential piece of business, burying themselves in spreadsheets and sales figures. It seemed almost irresponsible to be pushing skilled people out the door because of cultural fit. He called Anne.

"I'm not sure it's working," he said. "We're not where I want us to be, and I'm afraid the positives we were hearing from employees are all just lip service. What if, after everything we've put into this, we just drift back to the way it was before?"

Anne agreed that his concerns could be valid. With a change of this magnitude, backsliding was always a possibility. She suggested a survey of the employees and clients to see whether they felt the same way John did—that Purpose just wasn't working.

They posed a few questions to all of their employees and clients, expecting to hear that most people were still just doing business as usual. The results were beyond reassuring—they were staggeringly positive.

"I love coming to work and knowing that I am part of creating better leadership in the world," wrote one employee.

"Management has cleared the way for me to do the best possible job," wrote another.

From one employee came two gems: "The energy in our office is palpable" and "My department now says 'TGIM'—thank goodness it's Monday."

It was clear to the leadership team that the language within the company had changed, employees had begun to understand the company's *why*, and they were engaged with making it a reality.

And the clients' responses were even better, feeding back their enjoyment of working with Moguls, Inc. and their renewed sense of partnership.

"I've pointed several peers to Moguls because I know you're not worried about a finders fee or nonsense training—you're just passionate about putting great leaders where they belong," one client said.

And the most telling of all: "I never want to work with anyone but Moguls, Inc. to find and train my executives."

The responses re-energized the executives, providing them with the fuel to stay the course. They realized they had slipped into old habits and needed to trust in the power of their Purpose and stay resolute to their core values.

Five years after launching into Savage Thinking, Moguls, Inc. was the focus of a half-page article in the *New York Times*. John was speaking at conferences across the country on how Moguls, Inc. had made great leaders and leadership possible around the world by committing to a Purpose larger than protecting its own interests.

Allison transitioned smoothly into leadership at the firm, driven by the FOCUS statements she helped craft. She scheduled bi-weekly meetings with the entire executive team for the foreseeable future to ensure regular check-ins on how each area of the company was delivering on its Purpose.

And since undertaking these efforts to become a purposeful brand—in addition to John's being able to transition most of his time to working outside the day-to-day business and leaving Allison at the helm, the improvements in employee recruitment and retention, the more engaged and positive workforce, the more loyal clients who desired true partnerships with the company, and the goodwill garnered from the community—the company's profits have grown every year.

PART SIX

Future

Chapter 17

———

Where Do You Go from Here?

AT THE BEGINNING OF THIS BOOK WE DISCUSSED CURRENT CHAL-
LENGES FACING CORPORATE AMERICA. WE TALKED ABOUT THE TWO
GENERATIONS PUSHING FOR BETTER AND MORE MEANINGFUL WAYS
TO CONDUCT BUSINESS. WE INTRODUCED OUR APPROACH TO IMPROV-
ING THE BUSINESS WORLD—BY BEING CONSCIOUS OF THE WAKE BEING
LEFT BEHIND. AND WE SHARED THE IMPORTANCE OF CREATING A
PURPOSEFUL BRAND THAT STANDS FOR SOMETHING RELEVANT—ONE
THAT FINDS AND KEEPS ENGAGED EMPLOYEES, ATTRACTS AND
RETAINS LOYAL PARTNERS AND CUSTOMERS AND, IN DOING SO, GEN-
ERATES A POSITIVE IMPACT ON THE WORLD AND ON THE BOTTOM
LINE.

At this point, you might be thinking that you are already aware of
and know much of the material we discussed. If that is the case,
you could benefit from reading the following story about the critical
difference between knowing and doing, as mentioned in the Preface of
this book.

When we speak to companies about connecting with their Purpose and acting on it, we usually get a lot of nods. Most everyone in the audience is with us. Nothing we say startles or offends them. We all know the basics of what we think these corporate messages are.

Toward the end of our talk we tell them we know how to do a backflip. They perk up; this is different.

We begin to explain the mechanics. We explain that you start in a standing position, bend your knees, then swing your arms back up while pushing off the ground. Then you pull your body into a tuck, make a 360-degree revolution and land back on your feet, without your hands, head, or bottom touching the floor. The key is to get momentum from your arms and legs and to curl into a tuck position. Once the hips are past vertical, gravity will bring them back down.

Then we begin to stretch on the stage, prepping for the big flip. "We'll only do this once, so if you're in the back and can't see, you might want to stand up," we say. "Also, we'd appreciate it if someone would keep their thumb on 911." The audience grows visibly nervous.

We crouch; the audience holds its breath... we leap into the air—but do not do a backflip. With obvious relief, the people in the room laugh. Here's the problem, we tell them. We know how to do a backflip. But to actually do a backflip would require study and training. It would require hours and hours of attempts and failure and frustration.

Delivering on a compelling corporate Purpose, mission, vision, values, and behaviors is the same way. You know how to do it. You've read books and been to seminars and brainstormed and strategized. But to actually deliver value and meaning to all stakeholders requires a full commitment. Execution means every employee, top down, is aligned with your FOCUS and is working toward it. It means having an unwavering belief that it's the best direction for the company. It requires an investment of time, money, and hard work—and you will probably stumble and fall several times before feeling comfortable with your progress.

Maybe you know how to do a backflip. But are you committing to the execution? Ultimately, if you want to have a successful, purposeful brand, your company is going to have to leap off the ground, tuck, and land it.

You've made it through the book, which means you now have the knowledge of how to "do a backflip"—that is, how to uncover, align with, and begin building your brand on Purpose. You hopefully appreciate the power of this work and are ready to find your FOCUS, apply your FILTER, and begin to FUSE all your words and actions. But, of course, now the real work begins.

We have thrown a lot of things at you in this book, from history lessons to group-building exercises to treatises on the value of good storytelling. Ultimately, though, there's one key takeaway—creating an impactful and enduring company necessitates getting your head out of your bottom line and building your brand on Purpose.

> Purpose drives performance.
> Performance drives profits.

If you're interested in creating a purposeful brand, start thinking about how you can get your top leadership in a room and uncover that non-monetary reason for existence that's driving your company. If this book inspires you to do only one thing—it should be to find your Purpose and use it to inspire others!

In the remaining pages, you'll find resources and ideas for continuing what's been started here. Please explore; find the exercises that work best for your company, and begin building your brand on Purpose today.

Appendix A: Exercises

FIVE QUESTIONS IN FIVE MINUTES

———

Exercise
Ask each of your key executives to answer the following five questions. Give yourselves five minutes to write the answers.

- ❓ What is the one guiding principle that influences all your company's innovations, investments, and decisions?

- ❓ In one sentence, can you describe the main Purpose your company serves?

- ❓ In what ways does your company behave differently from any other business in your field?

- ❓ What percentage of your employees do you believe know what your organization stands for? What percentage of your customers?

- ❓ How would you place the following stakeholders in order of their importance to your company? *(choose only those applicable to your business)*:

  _____ Analysts
  _____ Board of Directors
  _____ Community
  _____ Customers
  _____ Employees
  _____ Shareholders
  _____ Suppliers

Once all of the responses are gathered and analyzed, you should get a preliminary understanding of what your executives believe makes the company tick, along with a strong indicator of the need for clarification or change. *(Explanation & Analysis on next page.)*

Explanation & Analysis

Five Questions in Five Minutes—This exercise helps you determine whether you already have a well-identified Purpose that is alive in your company. It also serves as a solid benchmark to compare against as your Purpose initiative moves forward. Run this exercise every year to track progress.

Below are some of the most common answers to the five questions.

❶ For many companies, the guiding principle that comes back most frequently is either "growth" or "profit." It's a telling answer because it says that it is more important to make money than to establish a meaningful relationship with customers and employees.

❷ Answers to the one-sentence summary question can vary. Many times profit, growth, or shareholder value are mentioned here, but if the company has a well-known mission or vision statement, some may parrot this.

❸ For many companies, this is the hardest question to answer. Most try to differentiate based on "price," "value," "quality," or their "people." The key word in the question is "behave," and none of these necessarily describe a differentiating behavior. Ideally, this sentence should be unique from anything a competitor would write.

❹ This is an excellent indicator of how well executives believe their communications are permeating their internal and external audiences. Respondents who answer with a low percentage suggest that the company's messages aren't currently well understood—which leaves opportunity for improvement.

❺ Establishing the way executives see the company by prioritizing its stakeholders is an important indicator of the company's priorities and values. If analysts and shareholders top the list, there's a good chance the company is forsaking better relationships with employees or customers for a bump in stock price or quarterly returns.

THE COMPANY DRIVERS

Exercise
Take 30 minutes to answer these ten questions:

- ❓ What makes our company tick?
- ❓ What are the intentions behind our policies and procedures?
- ❓ Why are customers/clients attracted to our business?
- ❓ Why are employees joining and leaving our company?
- ❓ Why should investors trust our company with their money?
- ❓ Which of our company's values are visible inside the business today?
- ❓ What drives our operations?
- ❓ Who leads and models the culture of the company?
- ❓ Who are the influencers within our company— the people trusted by our employees for information?
- ❓ What is our company fanatical about and how does this differentiate us?

Explanation & Analysis

The Company Drivers—This set of questions is designed to help you further examine the current landscape. You are looking for clear, cohesive answers that are consistent from all the respondents. If you see a lot of disparity in the answers, more work is needed. If the answers are similar, but most point solely to bottom-line focus, more work is needed.

These answers can also serve as a benchmark for you as you move forward through the Savage Thinking process. Retake this exercise once you have completed the entire process to determine if you have achieved:

- ❶ A closer consensus among the respondents
- ❷ More purposeful answers to the questions

These are indicators of whether your company's culture is improving and getting closer to delivering on your Purpose.

ENDEARING TRAITS

Exercise

You might consider questions similar to those posed in the book, *Firms of Endearment* to identify companies that people love:

- ❓ Would most people say that the world is a better place because our company exists?

- ❓ Do we have intensely loyal customers?

- ❓ How high is our employee turnover?

- ❓ Do we have a reputation for squeezing our suppliers?

- ❓ Do communities welcome us when we try to enter or expand?

- ❓ Do we have a record of environmental violations?

- ❓ How do we respond to industry downturns?

Explanation & Analysis

Endearing Traits—All of these questions can be quantified and measured over time to help you make more Purposeful decisions. Compare your answers to these questions every year to help you measure your transformation.

HIGH-PROFILE PURPOSE MATCHING

———

Exercise

Take 5—10 minutes to match the Purpose statements on the left with the correct company in the right-hand column.

A. We believe business can and must be a force of good in the world—and that this is also good for business

B. To shape the health and wellbeing of current and future generations

C. To bring joy to the lives of our customers, whether they are kids or kids at heart

D. To bring inspiration and innovation to every athlete in the world

E. We see a world in which everyone in America has the chance to go and see and do things they've never dreamed of—where everyone has the ability to fly

F. To help bring creative projects to life

G. To organize the world's information and make it universally accessible and useful

H. Empowering people to stay a step ahead in life and in business

_____ 1. **Nike**

_____ 2. **Google**

_____ 3. **Virgin Unite**

_____ 4. **Kickstarter**

_____ 5. **ING Direct**

_____ 6. **Jamie Oliver Food Foundation**

_____ 7. **Toys "R" Us**

_____ 8. **Southwest Airlines**

(Explanation & Analysis on next page.)

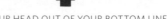
Explanation & Analysis

High-profile Purpose Matching—The correct answers are:

A. Virgin Unite
We believe business can and must be a force of good in the world—and that this is also good for business[1]

B. Jamie Oliver Food Foundation
To shape the health and wellbeing of current and future generations[2]

C. Toys "R" Us
To bring joy to the lives of our customers, whether they are kids or kids at heart[3]

D. Nike
To bring inspiration and innovation to every athlete in the world[4]

E. Southwest Airlines
We see a world in which everyone in America has the chance to go and see and do things they've never dreamed of— where everyone has the ability to fly[5]

F. Kickstarter
To help bring creative projects to life[6]

G. Google
To organize the world's information and make it universally accessible and useful[7]

H. ING Direct
Empowering people to stay a step ahead in life and in business[8]

This exercise is used to provide examples of powerful company statements and illuminate the difference between typical uninspiring mission statements and those that aspire to have real impact on the world.

PEER PURPOSE MATCHING

———

Exercise

This exercise should be set up exactly the same way as the preceding *High-profile Purpose Matching* exercise, but it will be tailored to your specific company and your industry.

On the left, you will have 8—10 Purpose statements (or the closest equivalent, which may be a mission statement, vision statement, or even just copy from About Us or Company History pulled from websites) of your own company and your key competitors in the industry. In the right column, you should list those companies.

Ask participants to take 5 minutes to match the "Purpose" statements on the left with the companies on the right.

Explanation & Analysis

Peer Purpose Matching—Participants often find this exercise much more challenging than the *High-profile Purpose Matching* exercise. In many cases, even executives are unable to identify their own statement among their peers' because none of them resonate deeply.

The reason these two exercises are performed back-to-back is so that executives can see the difference between companies who are clear about what they stand for—those who live their Purpose so visibly that even outsiders can identify them at a glance—or those that either have no clear Purpose or do not share it.

This generally reveals a huge opportunity to become the company that stands out in an industry as a purposeful brand.

BRAND SYMBOL

_____

Exercise

For this exercise, you will need dozens of cards with simple, symbolic, and iconic images on them that convey an idea, event, feeling, attitude, or personality from a historic, current, or future context. A few examples would be hands holding a globe, a child lifting a trophy, an old woman with her hands over her face, a runner breaking through the finish line tape, a bridge, an iconic athlete, a pop culture sensation, or a historic milestone. These should be images that can be interpreted in many different ways, but that all trigger some sort of visceral emotion. If you don't have someone to make the cards, consider bringing a variety of magazines into the room and having the team cut out images to discuss.

Spread these symbol cards out on a table where all participants can see and reach them. Then ask each person to choose one image in answer to each of these questions:

- ❓ Which image symbolizes our company today?
- ❓ Which image represents a vision of the desired future state of this company in five years?

Once everyone has made a card selection for each question, ask the participants to explain why they chose their specific images and what each card says about the company.

Explanation & Analysis

Brand Symbol—This exercise may bring up some surprising answers. By asking people to answer in the form of an image, you get their creative juices flowing. Often, very robust discussions happen during this exercise.

Be sure to have someone in the meeting noting both the symbols chosen and the interpretations of them. These are valuable insights into the way participants feel about the company and its future.

THE FIVE *WHYs*[9]

———

Exercise

This exercise is best done in a group setting. Use a whiteboard to capture this activity.

In order to understand the root motivation for your company, ask *why* multiple times. It generally takes approximately five *why* questions to get to the heart of the matter.

Start with a descriptive statement about your company. For example, we make _____ or we deliver _____.

Once an answer is shared, then ask *why* is this important? This question should be repeated until you get to the true root of what's driving the company. Continue asking *why* until there is an *aha* moment, or until asking *why* continually leads to the same answer.

EXAMPLE

We begin with the statement,

"We make automation software for manufacturing facilities."

❶ **Why do we make automation software?**
   Because automation can improve efficiency and safety for companies

❷ **Why focus on manufacturing facilities?**
   Because the manufacturing industry is very focused on upgrading its outdated technology and processes

❸ **Why are they upgrading?**
   Because manufacturing facilities have many legacy systems that are both more dangerous and less efficient than today's technology

❹ **Why do we want to help with these upgrades?**
   Because we want to help manufacturing companies achieve safer, more efficient performance

❺ **Why do we want that for manufacturing companies?**
   Because we value the safety of their people and we want our customers to be successful

Now the discussion is becoming more meaningful, touching on things that can actually lead you to your Purpose as a company.

(Explanation & Analysis on next page.)

Explanation & Analysis

The Five Whys—This is our adaptation of *The Five Whys*, invented in the 1930s by Sakichi Toyoda, innovator and founder of the company that became Toyota Motors.

While this exercise is traditionally used to solve a problem, we use it here to peel away layers of trite rhetoric and drill down to the source of what is driving your company.

Some answers that come out of this exercise may be true, but not helpful. For example, "By doing this very well, we will provide exceptional returns to all our stakeholders." Answers like these are still several levels of *why* away from the heart of the matter. Keep digging.

SENSORY VISION BUILDING

———

Exercise

For this exercise, gather key stakeholders in a room and dedicate approximately two uninterrupted hours.

Write these categories on a whiteboard:

- ⊛ **What you see**
- ⊛ **What you hear**
- ⊛ **What you say**
- ⊛ **What you feel**

Answering questions that correspond to each of the four categories is a good way to add texture to your vision statement:

1. In five years, what will you see when you walk into your offices? (location, space, jobsite, etc.) Encourage participants to be specific.

2. What will you hear others—employees, clients, visitors—saying? What's the buzz... the hum? Does it make you want to work here? Does it make you proud? Do you want to share this with the world?

3. What will you be saying to a guest, fellow employee, or client about your company? What kind of language will you use? How will you describe the company you have become? How is this any different from what you are saying today?

4. How do you feel when standing in your offices, space, location, jobsite? What kind of emotional connection do you have here?

(Explanation & Analysis on next page.)

Explanation & Analysis

Sensory Vision Building—This simple brainstorming helps to add texture and depth to your vision statement. The answers serve as the springboards for ideas that can shape future communications.

Let's assume you created a powerful vision statement during the uncovering of your FOCUS. Now you want to engage your stakeholders and inspire them with a strong desire to help you reach your mission and achieve your goals. In order to get your vision off the paper and infuse it into your culture, you need to make it aspirational, make it inspirational, and make it sensory. This brainstorming helps you establish, in telling detail, what the experience of interacting with your company will look, feel, and sound like when you achieve your vision.

This exercise helps breathe life into your vision by connecting imagination with actions. While it is great to believe in something lofty and aspirational, it's the details that help bring your ideas to fruition.

UNCOVERING VALUES-BASED BEHAVIORS

―――

Exercise

Identify a handful of your top employees. Consider their performance, dedication, abilities, interpersonal skills, and whatever attributes best align with your FOCUS.

❶ Write three things that you admire about each exemplary employee

❷ Answer these questions:

> **?** Why did you hire this person?

> **?** Why would you be reluctant to let him or her go?

> **?** How would your business suffer without this person?

> **?** Which of his or her behaviors would you like to see in other employees?

❸ From your responses, begin extrapolating a set of behaviors that are already part of your ideal employee's day-to-day life at the company

Explanation & Analysis

Uncovering Values-based Behaviors—By basing your decision on which behaviors align with your FOCUS and your top employees are already demonstrating, you ensure that the behaviors you choose are realistic and authentic to your culture—as they represent the best of the best. As part of a larger discussion about what behaviors are required for your company to deliver on the promise of its Purpose, this exercise can help you choose concrete, actionable behaviors to incorporate into your company's FOCUS.

Note: This same exercise can be used to clarify ideal clients and suppliers.

MINIMAL VALUES ELIMINATION
Exercise

——

This exercise is best done in a group setting. Use a whiteboard to capture this activity.

Start by writing as many single words as you can to describe your company. Write until no new words are added. Wait until everyone has exhausted his or her list and all words are captured on the board.

Once the board is covered, begin grouping similar words and remove duplicates. Next, eliminate those words that are too common to differentiate your company. And finally, remove any words that are not strongly defended by someone in the room.

To help with your elimination, here is a list, created by Robert Ferguson at Forging Values, of the 17 most common "minimal values" shared by Fortune 500 companies[10]:

- Integrity
- Respect
- Excellence
- Responsibility
- Teamwork
- Innovation
- Achievement
- Fairness
- Care
- Passion
- Leadership
- Learning
- Customers
- People
- Safety
- Community
- Environment

Explanation & Analysis

Minimal Values Elimination—Too many companies settle for values that make them sound just like everyone else. Work to reduce your list down to three to seven values that are ownable by your company and help to set you apart from competitors. If you end up with Integrity, Teamwork, Safety, and Innovation, ditch your list and start over—you are not pushing yourselves enough.

Each of these words is too broad to differentiate one company from another. If you find your group clinging to one of these "values", force yourselves to dig deeper to express what the word actually means within your culture. Try to identify words that are more specific and memorable.

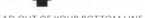
TESTING CREDIBILITY OF YOUR FOCUS

Exercise

In addition to the sample questions posed on pages 58 and 59, use the following for testing the credibility of your FOCUS with stakeholders.

Internal questions to consider:

- ❓ How long have you been with the company?
- ❓ What makes our company stand apart from competitors?
- ❓ Do you believe the company [insert restatement of Purpose]? If so, why do you believe that?
- ❓ How would you describe our culture?
- ❓ What one thing could be changed to make our culture better?
- ❓ If you could clone one aspect of the company to share with the world, what would it be?
- ❓ What would you say to convince someone to work here?
- ❓ Do you have the tools and training necessary for facing your day-to-day challenges?

External questions to consider:

- ❓ What is your current position?
- ❓ How long have you had a relationship with XYZ?
- ❓ What makes XYZ stand apart from their competitors?
- ❓ What is it about XYZ that made you decide to do business with them?
- ❓ Do you believe XYZ [insert restatement of Purpose]?
- ❓ If you could clone one aspect of XYZ and share it with the world, what would it be?

Explanation & Analysis

Testing Credibility of Your FOCUS—To attain the best results from these efforts, keep the interviews short. They can be conducted in person, on the phone, or online, but face-to-face usually provides superior results. This method leads to more of a conversation and the nuances of facial expressions and body language sometimes says more than mere words allow. To encourage candor, let participants know that names will not be attached to any of the information you receive. Use the feedback received from these interviews to help shape your messaging. And when making any announcements, remind people what they told you and show how this is invaluable in helping you deliver on your Purpose.

In most instances, it is best to have an outside party conduct this research so that the interviewees feel they can be open and honest.

EMPLOYEE ALIGNMENT

Exercise

Use the chart below and plot where each of your employees might fit with regard to how proficient each person is in his or her job and how well each aligns with your company's Purpose.

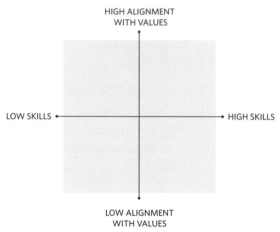

Explanation & Analysis

Employee Alignment—The ideal employee will fall into the upper right quadrant: highly skilled and closely aligned with your brand's Purpose. The second-most desirable employee is in the upper left quadrant, where the employee is highly aligned with Purpose and company values, but perhaps lacks certain skills or competencies.

While it is possible to move an employee from left to right on the graph by training him or her in additional skills that increase competency in his or her role, it is very challenging—if not impossible—to move an employee up on the chart.

An employee that is neither adequately skilled nor living your values is not a good fit for your organization.

The most challenging decisions are those that involve employees who fall into the quadrant with highly desirable skills but no clear alignment with Purpose. Create an actionable plan for how to address their poor alignment with Purpose. If they do not fit, they may be doing more harm than good.

CLIENT ALIGNMENT

——

Exercise

Consider charting your client base on an arc like this one to help you see the balance (or lack thereof) in your business. Use the arc to identify which customers are merely looking for the cheapest price and fastest turnaround, versus those more interested in a long-term relationship. The labels used here are for reference only. Write the terms that will work best for your business when performing this examination. Add your goals at the bottom so you can also track progress in this way.

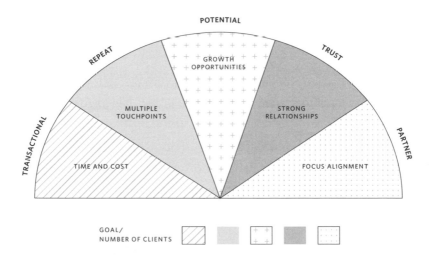

Explanation & Analysis

Client Alignment—This chart can help you assess, at-a-glance, your current balance of purposeful to non-purposeful clients and work. This makes it easier to lay the groundwork for moving your business forward in the direction of more purposeful engagements. And this is another metric that can be used for Purpose-based reporting.

FENCE SITTER IDENTIFICATION

—

Exercise

When instituting any change, you can divide your employees into three groups:

❶ Supporters—Those who embrace change

❷ Fence sitters—Those usually undecided about change

❸ Naysayers—Those generally in opposition to change

There are a few markers of a fence sitter that can help you identify those people to whom you need to pay extra attention during any evolution. This is not a one-time exercise, but rather guidelines and markers for what to look out for as you communicate with your people. Be sure to watch and listen closely, and identify those people who:

⭐ **Ask the most questions.** Often fence sitters will have immediate pushback to communications, in the form of questions.

⭐ **Want more information.** Those people who follow up afterward, looking for additional clarification, more documentation, and an explanation of how the leadership team came to its conclusions, are likely fence sitters.

After a meeting, they can be found gathering a group to engage in more dialogue. Fence sitters often want to talk to their peers about the changes, to hear both positive and negative perspectives, as part of their need for more information.

Explanation & Analysis

Fence Sitter Identification—Once you have identified fence sitters, stay close to this group. They can be the tipping point for any change initiative. When you engage them, answer all their questions and keep them informed; they will feel connected to the change and be more likely to support you.

Because of fence sitters' tendency to reach out to peers for information and perspectives, be sure that your supporters and influencers are well informed about the change and can provide positive reinforcement of your top-down messages. It is best to find ways to connect supporters with your fence sitters.

OUTSIDE-THE-CLASSROOM TRAINING

Exercise

Consider some of these "outside-the-classroom" training ideas:

❶ **Model problem-solving within the framework of your FOCUS**
Employees retain more when they participate and become engaged in the process.

❷ **One-on-one quizzes**
Get an idea of where employees stand in understanding your FOCUS without putting them on the spot in front of their peers.

❸ **Storytelling workshops**
Employees who can share the lore of your company will feel more comfortable talking about your culture and FOCUS.

❹ **Social media chatter**
Listen to and engage with the conversations employees are already having online. You can find a lot of teachable moments on social media, and it's a great place to gather stories.

❺ **Contests**
Healthy competition among employees can be a great motivator. Find ways to encourage them to prove to their peers how well they understand and live the company's Purpose.

❻ **Value recognition cards**
Give employees a way to acknowledge each other when they see your company values in action. Small handouts like collectible cards can easily be passed from one employee to another as recognition.

Explanation & Analysis

Outside-the-classroom Training—As with all of your training efforts, the goal is to engage employees in improving themselves, their knowledge and skills, and their contribution to the company.

By using fun and creative exercises, you keep this training from feeling like a burden. Instead, employees are engaged with the content and get more excited about the changes that Purpose is bringing to life in the company.

The training exercises suggested are just a few examples. We encourage you to brainstorm more ways to utilize the training platforms you already have in place to connect employees with your Purpose.

THE CULTURE TRAPS

Insight

Just as a cohesive culture can do great things for a business, a negative culture can sap the energy from employees and prime the company for failure.

As you go through this process, be careful to avoid the "culture traps"—the places where good intentions get derailed and either take off in an irrelevant direction or backslide into old legacy habits.

By avoiding these traps and living your story, you make your Purpose real both inside and outside the company. But keep in mind, just when you feel like you have a good handle on your culture, it's probably time to rinse and repeat your story again.

BEWARE OF THE CULTURE TRAPS THAT CAN TAKE YOU OFF THE PATH TO BECOMING A PURPOSEFUL BRAND

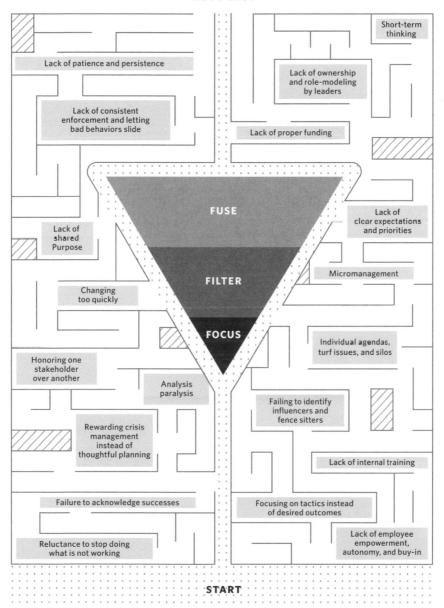

ADVOCACY

Short-term thinking

Lack of patience and persistence

Lack of ownership and role-modeling by leaders

Lack of consistent enforcement and letting bad behaviors slide

Lack of proper funding

FUSE

Lack of clear expectations and priorities

Lack of shared Purpose

FILTER

Micromanagement

Changing too quickly

FOCUS

Individual agendas, turf issues, and silos

Honoring one stakeholder over another

Analysis paralysis

Failing to identify influencers and fence sitters

Rewarding crisis management instead of thoughtful planning

Lack of internal training

Failure to acknowledge successes

Focusing on tactics instead of desired outcomes

Reluctance to stop doing what is not working

Lack of employee empowerment, autonomy, and buy-in

START

Appendix B: Finding Your Own Way

In the most productive workplaces, each person is aware of how to align his or her contributions with a larger shared Purpose. In order for that to happen, individuals must first understand their own personal Purpose.

Use the following exercises to help you get to a place of greater self-understanding so you can uncover and bring your personal Purpose to life.

10 REFLECTIVE QUESTIONS FOR SEEKING PERSONAL PURPOSE

- What gets me up in the morning?
  (other than an alarm clock or the kids)
- What brings me to work every day?
- What keeps me up at night?
- When am I most content at work?
- Who am I really serving?
- What am I doing when I am in flow*?
- What do I value most?
- If money were no object and failure wouldn't stop me, what would I be doing?
- What unique value do I bring to the world?
- What is the thing that would make me feel dejected and useless if I were told I could never do it again?

* Flow, sometimes called being "in the zone," is the mental state that occurs when you are performing an activity and are completely focused and immersed in it. It's a state of energy, creativity, full involvement, and enjoyment. When someone is in flow, they are completely absorbed in the activity, to the exclusion of all else.[1]

DISCOVER YOUR LIFE PURPOSE IN 20 MINUTES

This is the process recommended by Steve Pavlina[2]:

- ✪ Empty your mind of what others have told you.

- ✪ Sit in a quiet, relaxed place with no interruptions.

- ✪ Ask what your true Purpose in life is.

- ✪ Write whatever pops into your head.

- ✪ Keep writing until you write something that you have a strong emotional response to—that's your Purpose.

- ✪ Keep your answers short—just a few words.

- ✪ Persist until you get it.

- ✪ Don't give up too early, whether it takes 100, or 200, or 500 answers.

- ✪ Push past resistance. Don't view this as silly. It can be life changing.

- ✪ If you get stuck, take one-minute breaks to clear your mind and regain focus.

- ✪ You may find yourself writing the same thing over and over. Keep going.

- ✪ If you get a surge of many answers at once, highlight these and move forward.

- ✪ You may get irritated or frustrated. That's fine; this is part of the process.

- ✪ The real answer should produce a surge of emotions, and the final words should have a special energy for you.

- ✪ Ask yourself, if this were taken away from me, how would I feel? It should make you feel empty and lost.

USE THE FIVE *WHY*s TO UNCOVER PERSONAL MOTIVATIONS

In order to understand the root motivation for anything—a job, a life choice, a relationship, etc.—a person must ask, *why*? It takes approximately five *why* questions to get to the heart of the matter.

In this exercise, pose a question. Answer the question, then continue to ask *why* and answer four more times. Asking *why* five times gets past the surface reasoning and helps understand the core motivation.

EXAMPLE

❓ **Why am I spending my best working years at this company?**
Because this is the best place for me to earn a suitable living

❓ **Why is this the best place for me to earn a suitable living?**
Because my skillset matches the job

❓ **Why does my skillset match the job?**
Because I studied business in college

❓ **Why did I study business in college?**
Because my parents said I needed to do something reliable to support myself

❓ **Why did my parents tell me to do something reliable?**
Because they lived through tough times and didn't want the same for me

By repeating *why* five times, the asker uncovers the source motivation and can now decide to continue addressing his or her parents' fears or discover what he or she really wants to be doing for a living.

FINDING A PURPOSEFUL JOB

Ask this: Am I happy to be where I am each day, with people I respect, doing something of worth, for a company I care about? If the answer is yes, this is probably the right place for you to work. If the answer is no, it is time to do some soul searching and connect with what will help you fulfill your Purpose. Find a place where you can do this.

Questions to Determine Whether a Job is a Good Fit:

- ? Do I know my company's Purpose?
- ? Do I believe in that Purpose?
- ? Are my values in alignment with that Purpose?
- ? How does my job help me fulfill the need to be part of something bigger?
- ? Am I contributing in a way that inspires me?
- ? Does this job help me belong to something of significance?
- ? Am I able to contribute to the success of the company?
- ? Do I have enough autonomy to make a meaningful difference?

Appendix C: Three Steps of Storytelling

1. CAPTURE: **IDENTIFY A GOOD STORY**

Before you can begin using stories in your communications, you must first uncover them. So how do you find a story and identify its merits?

Begin by reviewing your Purpose, mission, vision, values, and behaviors. Identify the messages and attributes you want to share, both internally and externally. Write them at the beginning of a notebook or file called "Story Ideas."

If you've built your Purpose from something real and tangible within your company, you should begin seeing those stories all around your company, and they will grow and spread as your Purpose becomes more ingrained in your culture.

While it's vitally important for company leaders to model purposeful behaviors, your people will connect more deeply with your stories if they see themselves and their peers in them. Put a structure in place to gather stories from every level of your company.

Look for stories like these within your company:

- ⭐ You tried and failed to uncover some new method of delivery, then persisted to achieve success.

- ⭐ Summarize a project: the challenge, obstacles encountered, and your ultimate solution.

- ⭐ Things that got in the way and how you overcame problems with money, time, people, changes, etc.

- ⭐ Things looked bleak, and you took another route, persisted, and were victorious.

- ★ One person or group helped another achieve something that could not have been achieved alone.

- ★ Inspiration had run dry, and a new idea was hatched in an unusual way.

- ★ People were hoping you were going to achieve X, but you delivered X-plus.

Here's a business story example from Moguls, Inc.

One afternoon in late November, John learned that an employee had resigned and planned to start working for a competitor who was notorious for trying to poach Moguls best clients. John fumed as he processed the situation and knew he had to get out of the building to walk off some steam and think. He jammed the down button at the elevator bank, and rushed in so quickly when the doors opened that he almost knocked down a man standing inside. As the elevator slowly descended it suddenly lurched to a stop. The doors opened a few inches and froze in place—exposing only concrete wall. The two men pushed every button—nothing. They picked up the elevator phone—dead. They each tried their cell phones—no reception. In frustration, John leaned back against the wall and started laughing. Soon the other gentleman joined in. He introduced himself as Bob and explained that he was in the process of relocating his company. He had just leased space in this building and then found out that three of his executives would not be relocating with him. He was in a serious jam and needed to re-staff immediately to keep his company running. John smiled and said, "I just might be able to help you out with that problem." He told Bob about Moguls, Inc. Two hours later when the elevator technician finally freed them, the two men realized that getting stuck in an elevator on a day that each thought was a disaster, turned into a valuable business opportunity for both. Within two weeks John had placed three executives into Bob's company and the two became trusted business associates as well as friends.

Look for stories outside your company, in your day-to-day life, like these:

- ★ You learned about another company that rose to beat the odds.

- ★ Someone's family was helped through a tough time by the community.

- ★ The car you let into your lane at rush hour turned out to be driven by the CEO of a company you are trying to bring on as a client.

- ★ Your son learned a life lesson, and in turn you also were changed.

- ★ You ordered chicken and got tofu—a story you can connect with a customer situation when the wrong product was delivered.

Here's an example of how you might use a story from your life:

Growing up in my home, it was an understood rule that you did not ask my dad for help with your math homework. It wasn't because he was bad at math—quite the contrary! He was a brilliant mathematician—an algebraic topologist—one of a few dozen in the world at the time.

For those unfamiliar with this field let me explain it like this:

Algebraic topology is a branch of mathematics that uses tools from abstract algebra to study topological spaces. The basic goal is to find algebraic invariants that classify topological spaces up to homeomorphism, though usually most classify up to homotopy equivalence.

I know—that definition didn't really help me either!

*If you asked my dad a math question, it took forever for him to talk you through it because he was not just interested in your solving the problem, but also in understanding the **why** behind the solution.*

I made good grades in math, not because I was brilliant, but because it was expected in my house.

During my junior year in college I was struggling through a course in calculus. Halfway through the semester, I was totally lost and in serious jeopardy of failing the class.

So, the weekend before my midterm, I went home for a visit. While there, I casually mentioned my calculus dilemma to my dad. Within minutes, we were knee deep into unraveling my confusion.

He examined the solutions my professor was asking us to use and said, "Well, no wonder you don't get it. Let me show you a much more logical way to solve these equations."

*He proceeded to show me his method and explained **why** this made much better sense. I agreed. I got it! The light bulb went on, and I was ecstatic.*

The next week, I skipped in to my midterm exam, breezed through the test and confidently turned my paper in before the allotted time was up.

One week later, our graded exams were passed out in class. I made an F! What? How could that be?

I marched up to the professor after class, feeling certain that he had made a mistake. He agreed that all of my answers were correct, but argued that I had not used the methodology taught in class. He said that his assumption was that I must have cheated and I was lucky he was not kicking me out of his class.

I asked him if I could show him my method and he refused.

So I visited the dean of the math department's office and requested a meeting with the dean, my professor, and me.

Two weeks later, as the three of us gathered, I once again asked if I could share my solutions with the two of them. The dean said he trusted his staff and would not overrule the professor's grade.

That frosted my cookies! So I asked the two of them, "If you called up the chairman of the math department at Rice University and he corroborated my solutions, would you reconsider my grade?"

The two men sat with their arms crossed across their chests, smirked at each other, and agreed that, yes, that would satisfy them.

I said, "All right, here is his home phone number. Go ahead and call him. He's my dad!"

In the end, I passed calculus with a B-minus and was just grateful to get through the course.

*The important point here is that my understanding of **why** made the difference between my failing and passing the course.*

*Although many executives believe that their leadership style is "teaching" or "by example," it is important to make sure to share the **why** behind each message. This story shows how clarity and understanding affect behaviors and results.*

Great stories are not about when life goes smoothly, but rather about mistakes, failures, and small disasters. Look for times when a challenge is overcome—from dealing with traffic congestion to a major life-altering event.

Watch the world around you. Keep your eyes, ears, and mind open at all times because story-making events are happening every minute of every day. Pay attention to the subtext of what people say by listening beyond the words and focusing on the challenge encountered or frustration expressed.

Look for situations that showcase valor, sacrifice, pain, triumph, grit, shame, struggle, conflict, misunderstanding, growth, fear, failure, teamwork, imbalance, endurance, or tests of faith.

Write down your impressions immediately. Don't rely on your memory. Try to capture an event or incident in real time. It will be much more raw, authentic, and detailed. Rely on your "story notebook" or jot down the details wherever you take notes best.

Start making connections between the story, your life, your company, and your relationships. Think about your impressions of an event and determine your point of view. Think about how an event or incident might teach, encourage, support, or enlighten others. Focus on what others could learn from the story. Consider how sharing a situation helps someone else build a connection.

Of course, the moral of the story can be very flexible in order to fit the situation. For example, Kirk's story:

Kirk Whalum is a brilliant saxophone player. He practices for hours every day. Early in his career he was discovered by Bob James, a Grammy Award-winning jazz keyboardist, arranger, and producer. Mr. James was blown away the first time he heard Kirk play. Mr. James was instrumental in helping Kirk secure a recording contract, and soon thereafter, Kirk's career as a jazz saxophonist took off.

One afternoon, Kirk and another musician were discussing Kirk's busy schedule. The other gentleman observed, "Isn't it nice that you were in the right place at the right time and got lucky?"

Kirk said, "Let me tell you about luck. Luck is not being magically plucked out of obscurity by chance. Luck is being on a thousand street corners on a thousand different days, and being prepared when the call comes."

This story could be tied to several different messages:

- *It takes preparation and readiness to be able to take advantage of a lucky opportunity.*
- *We all make our own luck.*
- *Persistence wins in the long run.*
- *Talent alone is not enough—it's what you do with it.*

---

2. CRAFT: **BUILD THE STORY**

Now that you have gathered some potential company stories, what do you do with them? How do you take the situations you have identified and shape them into interesting events and lessons?

It helps to begin with an understanding of good story structure. The simplistic version of a story is this:

- ⊛ Life is good.
- ⊛ WHAM—life suddenly changes.
- ⊛ Someone rises to the challenge.
- ⊛ Wisdom is learned and shared.

This structure is familiar because we've all heard many great stories. We've been familiarized with the way stories are set up since we were old enough to have bedtime stories read to us.

However, it can be easy to get lost in the many sidebars and extra anecdotes that go with a story, and lose the tight structure of a good story when you're the one sharing it. Keep in mind a few key questions that your story needs to cover:

- ⊛ Who is the story about and why should we care about the hero?
- ⊛ What does this character want or need?
- ⊛ What is the transformation that takes place?
- ⊛ What enlightenment or skills does the hero gain?
- ⊛ How are the hero's beliefs changed?
- ⊛ What can be learned from this tale?

In the case of your company's stories, the "hero" may be you, another executive, an employee, a supplier, a particularly great customer, or your company as a whole. Regardless of whom is playing the leading role, you have to make your listener or reader connect emotionally.

Give your stories tension and infuse them with drama to help the listeners feel as if they are in the situation with the hero. Connect on a human level. Help listeners identify with the challenges your hero is facing and imagine themselves in the shoes of your character.

As you work on the story, write down as many details as you can think of. Work with the pieces of the story until you feel the flow is right and you have the right details to support the point you want to make. Then eliminate unnecessary details as you refine the narrative. Read it out loud, rearrange, rewrite, tighten, and continue to work until the structure is solid.

Refine. Edit. Repeat.

3. COMMUNICATE: **SHARE THE STORY**

The greatest story commandment? Make me care.

—Andrew Stanton[1]

While we are not all born storytellers, this craft can be learned. Most anyone can acquire the skills necessary for becoming a captivating storyteller. Just think back to when you were young and listened with rapt attention as your mom or dad read an exciting tale to you at night. The stories were simple, memorable, and most often connected to a message or moral. This is how we learned to navigate our world and get along with others.

One of the best ways to learn storytelling skills is to watch the masters. While these folks may look as if their tales are just naturally tumbling out, most have spent hours, days, or weeks perfecting their exact word sequence, inflection, phrasing, tone, and movements. They have rehearsed the story many times in order to learn which combinations of words work best for getting the reaction they are seeking. It only looks effortless because they have performed it so many times that they do not need to concentrate on the words anymore; instead, they can connect with the emotion.

We've listed a few of our favorite storytellers in Appendix D: Inspirations. Listen to a few to get a sense of different ways to weave a truly great story.

Spoken Stories

Here are a few tips for making your stories impactful:

⭐ **Keep it simple**

Make every word essential and every movement valuable. Too many adjectives can stop forward motion and leave listeners struggling to follow. Avoid run-on sentences. Don't babble, and try not to string together sentences connected by "and then." Say what you want to say with the fewest, most interesting, and most engaging words. Get rid of anything that does not move the story along.

⭐ **Let your passion flow**

Strive to help the audience "feel" the emotions of the main character(s). If you don't have passion for your story, neither will they. Help listeners quickly connect with why you are telling this story. For example, "On June 22, 2010, my life was forever changed with one small word." By letting people know that the story matters to you, you encourage them to care about it themselves.

⭐ **Build anticipation**

Don't give away your pearls of wisdom in the beginning of your story. Plant the suggestion that there are more and more exciting things yet to come. Help listeners wonder, "and then what?" "How will this be resolved?" Keep your audience on the edges of their seats. Build the suspense. Take them along on the journey with you.

⭐ **Make personal connections**

When speaking, try not to address the group as a whole. Instead, speak to individuals as if you are having multiple one-on-one conversations. Make each member of the audience feel a personal connection with what you are saying.

Deliver your story to one face at a time rather than scanning the room or talking to the back wall. Draw people in with eye contact and warmth that says, "I'm sharing this with *you*."

Train your executives and employees to be great storytellers. While you want your marketing department to handle the production of your communication materials, telling your company's stories is ultimately everyone's job.

Here are a few additional tips for becoming an effective storyteller:

- Practice your delivery, whether alone, in front of a mirror, on camera, to family, or with a small group.
- Show; don't just tell.
- Study body language so that you know what to do with your hands and body to add meaning to your stories.
- Don't pace around. Move with purpose.
- Focus on phrasing, timing, and expression.
- Understand that your strongest tools are silence and pauses.
- Trust your authentic voice. Speak like yourself; don't copy others.
- Believe that the story is more important than you. This eases nerves because it helps the audience be more focused on the story than on you.
- Watch the audience for engagement and reactions. Feed off of them.
- Don't rush. Take your sweet time without moving so slowly as to be boring.
- Practice, practice, practice, and practice some more.

Watching a great storyteller is like watching an Olympic ice skater. What has taken years of practice to perfect appears to the audience to be flowing and effortless. Don't lose heart or give up too quickly.

Written Narratives

For written stories, the steps are much the same as for oral stories. The main difference is that you are relying on your readers to create the voices, sounds, and actions in their heads. Your words alone need to bring readers' emotions along for the journey and help them believe in and care about the hero and the outcome. Be sure to help readers connect with the lesson learned.

When done well, your stories become your company folklore, empower all your stakeholders, and endure for generations.

If you need more convincing about the incredible power of stories in business, then look to the evidence or learn from a master.

Jonathan Gottschall—*The Storytelling Animal*
"Until recently we've only been able to speculate about story's persuasive effects. But over the last several decades psychology has begun a serious study of how story affects the human mind. Results repeatedly show that our attitudes, fears, hopes, and values are strongly influenced by story. In fact, fiction seems to be more effective at changing beliefs than writing that is specifically designed to persuade through argument and evidence." *(Jonathan Gottschall, author of The Storytelling Animal/Fast Company/http://www.fastcocreate.com /1680581/why-storytelling-is-the-ultimate-weapon)*

Robert McKee—*Story*
Read Robert McKee's book, *Story*, or sign up for one of his business "Storynomics" seminars. He is a master at teaching storytelling and has trained many great Hollywood screenwriters as well as numerous successful business leaders. *(www.storynomics.org)*

Appendix D: Inspirations

BOOKS

Conscious Capitalism
John Mackey and Raj Sisodia

Drive
Daniel Pink

Everybody Matters
Bob Chapman and Raj Sisodia

Firms of Endearment
Raj Sisodia, David B. Wolfe, and Jag Sheth

It's Not What You Sell, It's What You Stand For
Roy M. Spence Jr. and Haley Rushing

Start with Why
Simon Sinek

Taking People with You
David Novak

Uncontainable
Kip Tindell

SPEAKERS & STORYTELLERS

Shawn Achor
http://goodthinkinc.com/speaking/shawn-achor/

Brene Brown
http://brenebrown.com/

Simon Sinek
https://www.startwithwhy.com/

W Mitchell
http://www.wmitchell.com/

David Eagleman
http://www.eagleman.com/

Ray Kurzweil
http://www.kurzweilai.net/ray-kurzweil-biography

James Howard Kunstler
http://kunstler.com/

Dr. Anthony Atala
https://www.ted.com/speakers/anthony_atala

Grant Korgan
http://choosepositivitynow.com/about-us/grant-korgan/

Brian O'Malley
http://www.brianomalley.com/brianomalley/Motivational_
Speaker.html

Mark Sanborn
http://www.marksanborn.com/

Lori Nash Byron
http://famousinyourfield.com/about/

Roy Spence
http://www.itsnotwhatyousell.com/spence-about.htm

Jonathan Sprinkles
http://www.jsprinkles.com/

Andrew Davis
http://www.akadrewdavis.com/

ARTICLES

When Emotional Reasoning Trumps IQ
Roderick Gilkey, Ricardo Caceda, Clinton Kilts

VIDEOS

Life After Death by PowerPoint
Don McMillan

Culture Hacking at InfoQ and QCon
Floyd Marinescu

RESEARCH

Unrequited Profit: How Stakeholder and Economic Values Relate to Subordinates' Perceptions of Leadership and Firm Performance
Mary Sully de Luque, Nathan T. Washburn, David A. Waldman, Robert J. House

Notes

CHAPTER ONE

[1] "Global Desk: 2013 Edelman Trust Barometer," last modified January 20, 2013, accessed October 17, 2013, http://www.slideshare.net/EdelmanInsights /global-deck-2013-edelman-trust-barometer-16086761.

[2] Morten T. Hansen, Herminia Ibarra, and Urs Peyer, "The Best-Performing CEOs in the World," *Harvard Business Review*, January–February 2013, http://hbr.org /2013/01/the-best-performing-ceos-in-the-world.

[3] Steve Crabtree, "Northern America Leads the World in Workplace Engagement," *Gallup*, November 4, 2013, http://www.gallup.com/poll/165719/northern -america-leads-world-workplace-engagement.aspx.

[4] "BrainyQuote.com, Herb Kelleher," accessed January 20, 2016, http://www.brainyquote.com/quotes/quotes/h/herbkelleh575183.html.

[5] John Mackey and Raj Sisodia, *Conscious Capitalism: Liberating the Heroic Spirit of Business* (Boston, MA: Harvard Business Review Press, 2013), 19.

[6] "Peter's Laws: The Creed of the Persistent and Passionate Mind," Peter H. Diamandis' personal website, accessed October 17, 2013, http://www.diamandis .com/peters-laws/.

[7] "About Google," Google, accessed January 20, 2016, https://www.google.com /about/.

[8] "Who We Are: Manifesto," Acumen, accessed January 22, 2016, http://acumen .org/manifesto.

[9] "About Tesla," Tesla, accessed January 22, 2016, https://www.teslamotors.com /about.

CHAPTER TWO

[1] Francesco Guerrera, "Welch Condemns Share Price Focus," *Financial Times*, http://www.ft.com/intl/cms/s/0/294ff1f2-0f27-11de-ba10-0000779fd2ac .html#axzz3ATGiH5J3.

[2] "The Perils of Focusing on Short-Term Shareholder Value," Bill George website, accessed October 10, 2013, http://www.billgeorge.org/page/the-perils -of-focusing-on-short-term-shareholder-value.

3   Robert Schlesinger, "The Five Most Memorable Inaugural Addresses," *U.S. News & World Report*, March 12, 2009, http://www.usnews.com/opinion/slideshows /the-five-most-memorable-inaugural-addresses/5.

4   Michael S. James, "Is Greed Ever Good?," *ABC News*, August 22, 2002, accessed October 24, 2013, http://abcnews.go.com/Business/story?id=85971.

5   Hugo Martín, "Outdoor Retailer Patagonia Puts Environment Ahead of Sales Growth," *Los Angeles Times*, May 24, 2012, accessed July 28, 2014, http:// articles.latimes com/2012/may/24/business/la-fi-patagonia-20120525.

6   Jeff Rosenblum, "How Patagonia Makes More Money By Trying To Make Less," *Fast Company*, December 6, 2012, accessed December 7, 2012, http://www .fastcoexist.com/1681023/how-patagonia-makes-more-money-by-trying-to -make-less.

7   Shep Hyken, "Black Friday Disrupter: REI Goes Retail Rogue," *Forbes*, November 21, 2015, accessed January 18, 2016, http://www.forbes.com /sites/shephyken/2015/11/21/black-friday-disrupter-rei-goes-retail-rogue /#2715e4857a0b1e25af2d7e6f.

CHAPTER THREE

1   Leslie Wayne, "A Promise to be Ethical in an Era of Immorality," *The New York Times*, May 29, 2009, accessed October 24, 2013, http://www.nytimes.com/2009/05 /30/business/30oath.html?_r=0.

2   Ken Jacobson, "Whose Corporations? Our Corporations!," *AlterNet*, April 3, 2012, accessed October 10, 2013, http://www.alternet.org/story/154789/whose _corporations_our_corporations%21.

3   Daniel Pink, *Drive: The Surprising Truth About What Motivates Us* (New York: Penguin Group, 2009), 133.

4   Alexandra Levit, "Make Way for Generation Z," *The New York Times*, March 28, 2015, http://www.nytimes.com/2015/03/29/jobs/make-way-for-generation-z .html?_r=0.

CHAPTER FOUR

1   "Mission Statements: Mission Statement Examples: Company Mission Statements: General Motors," Samples Help!, accessed February 1, 2016, http://www.samples-help.org.uk/mission-statements/general-motors -mission-statement.htm; JLP, "Albertson's (ABS) Mission Statement," *Man On A Mission Blog*, June 25, 2005, accessed February 1, 2016,

http://manonamission.blogspot.com/2005/06/albertsons-abs-mission
-statement.html; "Company Information: Our Guiding Principles," Owen & Minor,
accessed February 1, 2016, http://www.owens-minor.com/companyinfo/values
/Pages/default.aspx; Glenn Grunenberger, "Would a Business Person Make a
Good President?" *Thoughts Before The Alarm Sounds Blog*, September 17, 2015,
accessed February 1, 2016, http://grunenberger.blogspot.com/; Jeffrey Abrahams,
*101 Mission Statements from Top Companies: Plus Guidelines for Writing Your Own
Mission Statement* (Berkeley, California: Ten Speed Press, 2007), 51; "Company
Mission Statements: Fortune 500 Mission Statements," MissionStatements.com,
accessed February 1, 2016, http://www.missionstatements.com/fortune_500
_mission_statements.html.

CHAPTER FIVE

1   Lisa Earle McLeod, "Think Profit is the Purpose? Think Again," *Talent Management*
(blog), September 20, 2012, http://talentmgt.com/articles/profit-is-not-a
-purpose.

2   "About Nike," Nike, accessed January 24, 2016, http://about.nike.com/.

3   "Microsoft Commitment to Accessibility: Mission & Strategy," Microsoft Accessibility, accessed January 22, 2016, https://www.microsoft.com/enable/microsoft
/mission.aspx.

4   "About Google," Google, accessed January 20, 2016, https://www.google.com
/about/.

5   Bruce Jones, "Mission Versus Purpose: What's the Difference?," *Talking Point: The
Disney Institute Blog*, April 23, 2015, https://disneyinstitute.com/blog/2015/04
/mission-versus-purpose-whats-the-difference/346/.

6   "About Dow: Our Company: Mission and Vision," Dow, accessed January 22, 2016,
http://www.dow.com/en-us/about-dow/our-company/mission-and-vision.

7   Rich Karlgaard, "Purpose-Driven Leadership," *Forbes*, July 23, 2009, http://
www.forbes.com/2009/07/23/bmw-hy-vee-karlgaard-intelligent-technology
-leadership.html.

8   Roy Spence, "Do-Gooders: How Business CEOs Find a Higher Purpose" Conscious
Capitalism video, 52:10, April 5, 2013, http://www.consciouscapitalism.org
/cc2013/video.

9   Ibid.

10 "BrainyQuote.com, Albert Einstein," accessed January 20, 2016, http://www
.brainyquote.com/quotes/quotes/a/alberteins133991.html.

CHAPTER SEVEN

1   "About: Our Organization," TED, accessed January 22, 2016, https://www.ted
    .com/about/our-organization.

2   "Virgin Unite," Virgin Group, http://www.virgin.com/unite.

3   "About Us," Bloom Energy, accessed January 22, 2016, http://www.bloomenergy
    .com/about/.

4   "Who We Are: Manifesto," Acumen, accessed January 22, 2016, http://acumen
    .org/manifesto.

5   "Our Ecoverse: Learn More: See Our Painted Picture," Maverick, accessed January
    21, 2016, http://maverickdna.com/Painted%20Picture2015.pdf.

6   "About Tesla," Tesla, accessed January 22, 2016, https://www.teslamotors.com
    /about.

7   "Working at Amazon," Amazon Jobs, accessed January 22, 2016, https://www
    .amazon.jobs/working/working-amazon.

8   Lisa Earle McLeod, "How P&G, Southwest, and Google Learned to Sell with
    Noble Purpose," *Fast Company*, 2012, http://www.fastcompany.com/3003452/
    how-pg-southwest-and-google-learned-sell-noble-purpose.

9   Patrick M. Lencioni, "Make Your Values Mean Something," *Harvard Business Review*,
    July 2002, https://hbr.org/2002/07/make-your-values-mean-something.

10 "About Google: Company: What We Believe: Google's Ten Things We Know
    to Be True," Google, accessed January 22, 2016, http://www.google.com/about
    /company/philosophy/.

11 "Our Foundation Principles," The Container Store, accessed January 22, 2016,
    http://standfor.containerstore.com/our-foundation-principles/.

12 "About Southwest: Careers: Culture," Southwest Airlines, accessed February 15,
    2016, https://www.southwest.com/html/about-southwest/careers/culture.html.

13 "Working Here: Culture & Diversity," Disney Careers, accessed August 28, 2014,
    http://www.disneycareers.com/en/working-here/culture-diversity/.

14 "About Us: Core Values," Blinds.com, accessed February 15, 2016, http://www
    .blinds.com.

CHAPTER NINE

1   "About: Our Organization," TED, accessed January 22, 2016, https://www.ted
    .com/about/our-organization.

2   "Working Here: Culture & Diversity," Disney Careers, accessed August 28, 2014, http://www.disneycareers.com/en/working-here/culture-diversity/.

3   M. Jackson Wilkinson, "The Customer Isn't Always Right, but the Customers Are Always Right," *Inspire, A Design & Interaction Blog*, April 1, 2008, https://viget.com /inspire/the-customer-isnt-always-right-but-the-customers-are-always-right.

CHAPTER TEN

1   Delphine Hirasuna, "Walt Disney's Creative Organization Chart," *@Issue: The Online Journal of Business and Design Blog*, August 7, 2009, http://www.atissuejournal .com/2009/08/07/walt-disney%E2%80%99s-creative-organization-chart/.

2   Phillip Elmer-DeWitt, "Rethinking Apple's Org Chart," *Fortune*, August 29, 2011, https://fortune.com/2011/08/29/rethinking-apples-org-chart/.

3   Jane L. Levere, "The Lemonade Stand that Umpqua Bank Built," *The New York Times*, July 16, 2007, http://www.nytimes.com/2007/07/16/business/media /16adnewsletter.html?8seia&emc=seia&_r=0; "Umpqua Life: News & Murmurs," Umpqua Bank, https://www.umpquabank.com/news-and-murmurs/complete -merger-04182014/.

4   "Blake Mycoskie's Bio," TOMS, accessed January 25, 2016, http://www.toms.com /blakes-bio.

CHAPTER ELEVEN

1   "What We Do: The Center for Innovation," Mayo Clinic, accessed August 28, 2014, http://www.mayo.edu/center-for-innovation/what-we-do/the-center-for -innovation.

2   Cameron Herold, *Double Double: How to Double Your Revenue and Profit in 3 Years or Less* (Austin, TX: Greenleaf Book Group Press, 2011), 10.

CHAPTER FOURTEEN

1   Simon Sinek, *Start with Why: How Great Leaders Inspire Everyone to Take Action* (New York: Portfolio, 2009), 40–41.

2   "American Rhetoric, Top 100 Speeches: Duty, Honor, Country," American Rhetoric, accessed January 26, 2016, http://www.americanrhetoric.com/speeches /douglasmacarthurthayeraward.html.

3   Mitch Joel, "Digital Storyteller," *Six Pixels of Separation–The Blog*, August 3, 2010, http://www.twistimage.com/blog/archives/digital-storyteller/.

4   John Mackey and Raj Sisodia, *Conscious Capitalism: Liberating the Heroic Spirit of Business* (Boston, MA: Harvard Business Review Press, 2013), 190.

5   Roland Barthes and Lionel Duisit, "An Introduction to the Structural Analysis of Narrative," *New Literary History* 6, No. 2, On Narrative and Narratives (Winter 1975), 237.

6   Ty Montague, "If You Want to Raise Prices, Tell a Better Story," *Harvard Business Review,* July 31, 2013, http://blogs.hbr.org/2013/07/want-to-raise-prices-tell -a-be/.

7   Ravi Sawhney and Deepa Prahalad, "The Role of Design in Business," *Bloomberg Business,* February 1, 2010, http://www.businessweek.com/stories/2010-02-01 /the-role-of-design-in-businessbusinessweek-business-news-stock-market-and -financial-advice.

8   Cheryl Conner, "How Design Matters—More Than Ever—In 2014," *Forbes,* December 1, 2013, http://www.forbes.com/sites/cherylsnappconner/2013/12/01 /how-design-matters-more-than-ever-in-2014/.

CHAPTER FIFTEEN

1   Simon Sinek's Twitter page, August 27, 2014, https://twitter.com/simonsinek /status/504645206961307648.

2   Joe Keohane, "How Facts Backfire," *The Boston Globe,* posted on Boston.com July 11, 2010, accessed August 28, 2014, http://www.boston.com/bostonglobe/ideas /articles/2010/07/11/how_facts_backfire/.

3   "About: History," Don't Mess With Texas, accessed January 22, 2016, http://www .dontmesswithtexas.org/about.

4   "Cases: From Top-Down To Bottom-Up," Innovisor, accessed January 28, 2016, http://www.innovisor.com/wp-content/uploads/2016/01/From-TOP-DOWN-to -BOTTOM-UP.pdf.

5   Mike Klein and Jeppe Vilstrup Hansgaard, "The Story of PR: Lessons From Lincoln," *Communication Director,* April 2012, http://www.communication-director.com /issues/new-pr-profile/lessons-lincoln#.Vp5d71MrKJZ.

6   Richard Daft, *Organization Theory and Design* (Thomson South-Western, 2007), 333.

CHAPTER SIXTEEN

1   Lisa Earle McLeod, "How P&G, Southwest, and Google Learned to Sell with Noble Purpose," *Fast Company,* 2012, http://www.fastcompany.com/3003452/ how-pg-southwest-and-google-learned-sell-noble-purpose.

2 Simon Sinek, *Start with Why: How Great Leaders Inspire Everyone to Take Action* (New York: Portfolio, 2009), 147.

3 Raj Sisodia, David B. Wolfe and Jag Sheth, *Firms of Endearment: How World-class Companies Profit from Passion and Purpose* (Wharton School Publishing, 2007), 19.

4 Daniel Pink, *Drive: The Surprising Truth About What Motivates Us* (New York: Penguin Group, 2009), 131–146, 208.

5 Nathan Furr, "How Failure Taught Edison to Repeatedly Innovate," *Forbes*, June 9, 2011, http://www.forbes.com/sites/nathanfurr/2011/06/09/how-failure-taught -edison-to-repeatedly-innovate/#4a8e760838f5.

6 Nanette Byrnes and Michael Ardndt, "The Art of Motivation," *Bloomberg Business*, April 30, 2006, http://www.businessweek.com/stories/2006-04-30/the-art -of-motivation.

7 Ken Iverson, *Plain Talk: Lessons from a Business Maverick* (New Jersey: John Wiley & Sons, Inc., 1997), 75.

8 "About Google: Careers: Life at Google: How We Hire," Google, accessed August 29, 2014, http://www.google.com/about/careers/lifeatgoogle/hiringprocess/.

9 Brian Womack, "Google Gets Record 75,000 Job Applications in a Week," *Bloomberg Business*, February 3, 2011, http://www.bloomberg.com/news/2011 -02-03/google-gets-75-000-job-applications-in-one-week-topping-record -set-in-07.html.

10 Bill Taylor, "Why Zappos Pays New Employees to Quit–And You Should Too," *Harvard Business Review*, May 19, 2008, accessed January 7, 2016, https://hbr .org/2008/05/why-zappos-pays-new-employees/.

11 "Employee-First Culture," The Container Store, accessed August 29, 2014, http://standfor.containerstore.com/our-foundation-principles/.

12 "Goodreads, Maya Angelou," Goodreads, Inc., accessed January 26, 2016, http://www.goodreads.com/quotes/663523-at-the-end-of-the-day-people -won-t-remember-what.

13 Susan Berfield, "Will Investors Put the Lid on the Container Store's Generous Wages? CEO Kip Tindell's brand of 'conscious capitalism' is being tested in the face of a plunging share price," *Bloomberg Business*, February 19, 2015, http://www.bloomberg.com/news/articles/2015-02-19/container-store -conscious-capitalism-and-the-perils-of-going-public.

APPENDIX A

[1] "Virgin Unite," Virgin Group, http://www.virgin.com/unite.

[2] "Jamie Oliver Food Foundation," accessed January 11, 2016, http://www
.jamieoliverfoodfoundation.org.uk/.

[3] "About Us: Vision & Values," Toys"R"Us Inc., accessed January 11, 2016,
http://www.toysrusinc.com/About-us/vision-values/.

[4] "About Nike," Nike, accessed January 24, 2016, http://about.nike.com/.

[5] Lisa Earle McLeod, "How P&G, Southwest, and Google Learned to Sell with
Noble Purpose," *Fast Company*, 2012, http://www.fastcompany.com/3003452
/how-pg-southwest-and-google-learned-sell-noble-purpose.

[6] "About Us," Kickstarter, accessed January 11, 2016, https://www.kickstarter.com
/about.

[7] "About Google," Google, accessed January 20, 2016, https://www.google.com
/about/.

[8] "About Us, Purpose & Strategy," ING, accessed January 11, 2016, http://www
.ing.com/About-us/Purpose-Strategy.htm.

[9] "5 Whys," Wikipedia, last modified December 4, 2015, accessed January 25, 2016,
https://en.wikipedia.org/wiki/5_Whys.

[10] Robert Ferguson, "17 Common Values," Forging Values, http://www.forgingvalues
.com/17-common-values/.

APPENDIX B

[1] "Flow (Psychology)," Wikipedia, accessed January 25, 2016, https://en.wikipedia
.org/wiki/Flow_(psychology).

[2] "How to Discover Your Life Purpose in About 20 Minutes," Steve Pavlina,
http://www.stevepavlina.com/blog/2005/01/how-to-discover-your-life-purpose
-in-about-20-minutes/.

APPENDIX C

[1] Andrew Stanton, "The Clues to a Great Story," TED video, 19:09, March 2012,
https://www.ted.com/talks/andrew_stanton_the_clues_to_a_great_story.

Index

Acknowledgments

WE WANT TO GIVE OUR FIRST AND MOST SPECIAL THANKS TO PAULA SAVAGE HANSEN, THE FOUNDER OF SAVAGE BRANDS, MAVERICK AND CHASER OF WILD IDEAS. SHE IS THE CONSUMMATE ENTREPRENEUR AND PIONEER IN OUR PROFESSION AND HAS BELIEVED FROM DAY ONE THAT WE CAN USE THE BUSINESS OF DESIGN TO CHANGE THE WORLD.

Everyone at Savage Brands has put tremendous faith, time, and energy into our Purpose. We literally could not have done it without their trust and belief. Our team has endured countless crazy moments, contributed unique perspective to our heated debates, and kept their chins up and smiles on through some of the hairiest times of transformation. We know that the journey continues to be worth it and we can't thank them enough for standing together—connectedness is truly our greatest strength. Two special shout-outs to Dahlia Salazar and Catherine Harris. There are no words to express how much their contribution to the thinking, design, and content of this book (as well as to their day jobs) was instrumental and appreciated.

Of course, we both want to thank our families for everything they have done for us over the past two years. It has come in the form of patience and the sacrifice of some serious time. We are blessed by them and so thankful that they believe in us. Thank you to Vistage Group 3627 for being a sounding board and helping shape and test our view on how great businesses are built and great leaders are formed.

All the talented authors that have pursued the topic of Purpose and Conscious Capitalism, and proven beyond a shadow of doubt that this is the optimum path, have our eternal gratitude. And, last but not least, thanks to all of the great visionaries and leaders that have put their faith in us and Savage Brands to take them through this process over the years—or even been open enough to just listen.

—Jackie and Bethany